ONCE A JOLLY
HANGMAN

ONCE A JOLLY
HANGMAN

ALAN SHADRAKE

THIS BOOK IS NOT FOR SALE OR IMPORT INTO SINGAPORE

First published in Malaysia in 2010 by GB Gerakbudaya Enterprise Sdn Bhd.
This revised and updated edition published in Australia and the UK in 2011 by
Pier 9, an imprint of Murdoch Books Pty Limited

Murdoch Books Australia
Pier 8/9
23 Hickson Road
Millers Point NSW 2000
Phone: +61 (0) 2 8220 2000
Fax: +61 (0) 2 8220 2558
www.murdochbooks.com.au

Murdoch Books UK Limited
Erico House, 6th Floor
93–99 Upper Richmond Road
Putney, London SW15 2TG
Phone: +44 (0) 20 8785 5995
Fax: +44 (0) 20 8785 5985
www.murdochbooks.co.uk

Text copyright © Alan Shadrake 2011
The moral right of the author has been asserted.

Cover design: Design by Committee, copyright © Murdoch Books Pty Limited 2011
Front cover image © spekulator/stock.xchng
Back cover image © Getty Images (top), © Mohd Fyrol/AFP/Getty Images (bottom)
Internal design copyright © Murdoch Books Pty Limited 2011
Production: Renee Melbourne

National Library of Australia Cataloguing-in-Publication entry

Shadrake, Alan
Once a jolly hangman / Alan Shadrake
978-1-74266-373-9 (pbk.)
Justice, Administration of—Singapore
Law—Political aspects—Singapore
Singapore—Politics and government
Dewey Number: 347.5957

Printed in Slovenia

CONTENTS

Part III: Scandalising the Judiciary

FOREWORD TO THE ORIGINAL EDITION

MARGARET JOHN

AMNESTY INTERNATIONAL

Alan Shadrake's book, *Once a Jolly Hangman*, is a timely contribution to growing criticism of Singapore's shameful use of the death penalty. Once dubbed by *The Economist* as the world execution capital, Singapore is believed still to have one of the highest per capita rates of execution of any country worldwide, thus remaining totally out of step in the move regionally and internationally towards a death penalty-free world. A historic momentum is building from which Singapore chooses to exclude itself.

Executions are no longer a matter exclusively internal to an individual country's criminal justice system. Executions are now squarely an international issue. A small but growing anti-death penalty group of Singaporeans along with international organisations are gaining an effective voice. Standards have now been set by the United Nations. The UN's 2008 resolution calling for a worldwide moratorium on executions as a step towards total abolition has been heeded by an increasing number of countries. Not so by Singapore, however. Over 420 people have been executed there since 1991, mostly for drug trafficking, for which there is a mandatory death sentence. A number of countries have mounted protests against the execution of their nationals in Singapore and cases have been raised at the highest level. The worldwide anti-death penalty campaign will not be deterred. Moreover, the struggle against executions also highlights Singapore's other human rights realities: the difficulties of acting in opposition to policies generally of the ruling People's Action Party, which has been in power over half a century; government control of the media and civil society organisations, thus curbing public debate and limiting independent monitoring of human rights; and restrictions on cause-related demonstrations.

Once a Jolly Hangman unearths new or little-known information. The author argues convincingly that only those cases with possible negative political or economic outcomes appear to have succeeded in preventing executions of foreign nationals. In contrast, he exposes the pitiful, hopeless situation of poor, uneducated or desperate drug mules with no important connections. Alan Shadrake's interviews with Singapore's executioner, Darshan Singh, provide eye-opener descriptions of actual executions. And he gives the reader insights into the efforts of Singapore's own small group of anti-death penalty campaigners, such as heroic lawyer and human rights activist M. Ravi, alongside whom we, on the outside, are privileged to work. And, importantly, the reader is brought close to the heart of the matter—to the anguish of the victims themselves.

Amnesty International sees the death penalty as the ultimate torture, cruel, inhumane and degrading, prohibited by international human rights standards. It is a view now shared by an increasing number of governments, as they become convinced executions are futile, do not solve crimes, have no particular deterrent quality, are more than likely to be imposed disproportionately on the marginalised in society, are irreversible, and may result in executing the innocent. Moreover, executions add to a culture of violence by making State violence an acceptable way of dealing with problems. Singapore's leaders cling to their outmoded arguments that there is no international consensus on the death penalty, that it is a deterrent, that it is used for only the most serious crimes, that it is not a human rights issue, that Singapore has a transparent and fair justice system, and that Amnesty International has got its facts wrong. They are arguments increasingly difficult to uphold in the face of world standards and trends.

Margaret John
Coordinator for Singapore and Malaysia
Amnesty International Canada

FOREWORD TO THE NEW EDITION

JULIAN BURNSIDE, QC

The government of Singapore does not want anyone to read this book.

When it was first published in Singapore, police raided Alan Shadrake's hotel room and arrested him. He was taken into custody and interrogated for two full days and two sleepless nights, then charged with contempt of court by 'scandalising the judiciary'. Kenneth Jeyaretnam, leader of the opposition New Reform Party, and son of lawyer and human rights campaigner, J.B. Jeyaretnam, wrote saying: 'I do believe there is a pact between the PAP [People's Action Party] and foreign journalists or foreign media corporations. The pact is you can come in and out freely and report but don't touch our economic miracle model or the systems of our fake democracy. It is a truly Faustian pact ...'

As Shadrake awaited trial, he discovered to his discomfort just what happens when a person challenges the Singapore system. He was followed everywhere. Journalist friends reacted with alarm if Shadrake called them from his mobile, concerned that their association with him would then be known to the police. They knew, although at first he did not, that his mobile phone was bugged by the police. Most local journalists did not have the stomach to be seen as opponents of the regime.

His trial in the Singapore Supreme Court started on Monday, 18 October 2010. At the heart of the prosecution was the allegation that Shadrake had committed contempt of court by saying (and, it must be said, illustrating by example) that there was 'something sinister: how the Singapore legal system works in secret and how politics, international trade and business often determine who lives and who dies on the gallows'. The examples he gives point fairly strongly in support of that conclusion.

The prosecutor, after citing numerous passages from the book, said: 'These passages allege or insinuate that the punishments meted out by the Singapore Judiciary for drug-related offences depend on whether the accused is wealthy, from a privileged background or is well-connected in Singapore society' and that '[Shadrake] insinuates that the Singapore Judiciary is a tool of the People's Action Party to muzzle political dissent in Singapore ...' In one sense she was right: those charges can be levelled at the system in Singapore. The force of Shadrake's book is that in case after case he piles up evidence to support his critique of the way the system works in Singapore.

Shadrake's book reminded me immediately of time I spent in Singapore some years ago, teaching advocacy to Singapore lawyers (alongside J.B. Jeyaretnam, as it happens). The striking thing about those lawyers in Singapore was that so many of them were unwilling to stand up to the Court: they acted as if any criticism of any aspect of the system was unthinkable. But these are the people whose role it was to stand between the State and the individual. The impression I formed then of the cowed compliance of many (but not all) Singapore lawyers has never left me, and it is confirmed by this book.

Shadrake's book is about the use of capital punishment in Singapore. The Jolly Hangman, Mr Singh, takes pride in his work. He is after all only a servant of the State, doing the State's bidding. It is a reminder of some hard truths about capital punishment.

Capital punishment is the cold-blooded killing of a person by the power of the State. Let us not flinch from this: after investigation, trial and appeals, after all passion is spent, the State coldly, deliberately snuffs out a human life. Albert Camus brilliantly illustrated this point in his 1957 essay 'Reflections on the Guillotine':

An execution is not simply death. It is just as different from the privation of life as a concentration camp is from prison. It adds to death a rule, a public premeditation known to the future victim, an organization which is itself a source of moral suffering more terrible than death. Capital punishment is the most premeditated of murders, to which no criminal's deed, however calculated, can be compared.

There are those who turn to holy scriptures for guidance in these matters. To justify the execution of murderers, they turn to the Sixth Commandment: Thou shall not kill. It is one of the most basic moral lessons and the most universal. Not surprising perhaps, given the individual self-interest we all have in its being a general rule. But capital punishment breaks this rule just as surely as murder does.

Australians reacted sharply to the execution of Van Nguyen Tuong, an Australian citizen executed in Singapore on 2 December 2005. His is one of the stories Shadrake tells. Public sentiment in Australia against hanging Van Nguyen showed how far we had matured since the days, forty years ago, when Barry Jones led a campaign to prevent the State of Victoria from executing Ronald Ryan. But it is not quite so simple. Many Australians supported the idea of executing Saddam Hussein; John Howard as Prime Minister wanted to see the Bali bombers executed.

By similar logic, Singapore justifies its use of capital punishment on utilitarian grounds: the government says that the drug problem in Singapore would be much worse if those caught smuggling drugs, as Van Nguyen was, were not killed by the State. How curious then that this logic does not extend to cases where Singapore's diplomatic or trade interests are involved.

That is the puzzle Shadrake's book seeks to answer. Singapore's response suggests that the answer has hit a raw nerve.

Julian Burnside
Melbourne, 2011

PREFACE

I never imagined that I would one day go to Singapore, write a book about its revered but much-feared Chief Executioner and its justice system—and then end up in the dock myself.

The story began when I was invited by the Singapore Tourism Board to write a travel feature to tempt Americans to visit the city-state. Singapore's bird park, its orchid garden, the legend of the Merlion, and historic hotels like Raffles or the Fullerton were not the kinds of topic I usually covered. The trip lasted only a week but, having an inquiring mind, I soon had the feeling that I would never discover the true nature of this bland, authoritarian nation from a tour like this. Everything seemed too clean, too efficient and just too damned perfect for my way of thinking. It reminded me a little of the Hollywood movie, *The Stepford Wives*.

I flipped through the pages of Singapore's biggest daily newspaper, the *Straits Times*—which I soon discovered was mockingly called the 'Straits Jacket' on account of its skill at repressing all ideas other than those approved by the ruling People's Action Party. Suddenly I found myself following a sinister trail involving murders, drug trafficking and police corruption that began in the city-state and snaked around the world, linking Great Britain and Australia in a series of dramas I also became enmeshed in.

It started with what became known as the Orchard Towers Murders. There were two suspects: a British millionaire financial adviser and his Chinese girlfriend who fled to England and then

Australia. Around the same time, a young man named Nguyen Van Tuong, an Australian citizen, was about to go on trial for heroin trafficking; it seemed inevitable he would end up on death row. In fact, his execution was to stir anti-death penalty campaigners across Australia and threaten a major rift with Singapore.

Many months later I decided to return from my home in Las Vegas and keep tabs on both these cases. An interview with the prison officer who had been Singapore's Chief Executioner for almost fifty years, indeed since colonial days, was also on my mind. It was a daunting quest but after months of relentless searching I managed to find Darshan Singh, the man who had reputedly hanged an estimated 1000 men and women, mainly for murder and drug trafficking. Even more surprisingly, I got him to talk. This led to a meticulous search of legal files and archived cases going back to 1963. At the same time, I interviewed abolitionists and lawyers who had been involved in sensational cases that had been largely under-reported or not reported at all. The result was a unique glimpse into the deadly career of arguably the most prolific executioner who ever lived—a man who sincerely believes he has played a pivotal role in keeping Singapore one of the safest places on earth. And I discovered something else, something sinister: how the Singapore legal system often works in secret and how politics, international trade and business can determine who lives and who dies on the gallows.

I am often asked—and often wonder myself—how and why I got involved in all this in the first place. At times it was as though a mysterious, unseen power was driving me on. Then again, although this may seem ridiculous to many, it may all have come about as the result of a curse—in particular, a curse uttered by another victim of Singapore's dreaded gallows, Vignes Mourthi, just before he was hanged by Singh. Mourthi was being bundled from the court when the Chief Justice, Yong Pung How, dismissed lawyer Ravi's last-ditch attempt to save him with the words, 'You had better say goodbye to him. That's all you can do.'

Said Ravi: 'I last saw his face as he disappeared down a stairway leading from the dock. He looked up at me and said: "I have put a curse on Singapore. They will never forget what they have done to me."'

I do not usually have nightmares but soon I began experiencing 'visitations' in which mysterious, distorted, unrecognisable faces pressed in on me, swirling around, coming ever closer as if trying to suffocate me before drifting away. It was a disturbing experience, the like of which I had never had before. On one occasion I struggled desperately to wake up. It was like being sucked back into a whirlpool. Then I was wide awake, troubled and trembling, wondering what it all meant. Once calm, I closed my eyes and drifted off, only to be confronted again by these distressed faces coming ever closer and just as frightening as before. Was this one of those 'message' dreams that I occasionally had in my childhood—dreams that had come true? If so, what was it all about? The 'answer' came to me in a flash. Perhaps those haunting faces were those of the many lowly drug mules and other unfortunates who had been condemned to death and hanged. They were always on my mind —Flor Contemplacion, the slave-driven maid; Amara Tochi, the Nigerian kid who dreamed of soccer stardom; Shanmugam Murugesu, Angel Mou Pui-Peng and many others who were lured to their deaths while the leaders of the drug syndicates escaped any kind of punishment. Were these the same faces I had seen in that disturbing nightmare? Was this a visitation from the spirit world, all of them urging me to carry on the fight, bring them justice? No one will ever know.

Alan Shadrake
Singapore, February 2011

INTRODUCTION

SINGAPORE'S SECRETS

Woodlands. It seemed an unlikely part of Singapore to find the home of the hangman. Named after the vast acres of rubber trees planted by the British during early colonial days when Singapore was a mosquito-infested mango swamp, Woodlands lies just across Johor Strait from the southernmost tip of the Malaysian peninsula. It is a quiet, peaceful area, removed from Singapore's characteristic hustle and bustle. But there I was driving along Upper Bukit Timah Road, trying to feel optimistic that the address I had found was the right one. Or, more to the point, that the man who lived there really was Singapore's Chief Executioner, Darshan Singh. I wanted to meet this unknown but much-feared gentleman who was about to hang the Australian drug trafficker Nguyen Van Tuong, then on death row in Changi Prison. The imminent execution of Nguyen was promising to create a storm of protest across Australia and many parts of the world.

I was new to Singapore in 2003 and it was the first time since capital punishment was abolished in Britain that I had lived in a country where the death penalty seemed to be almost universally accepted. At that time the trial process had not been completed, but it seemed a foregone conclusion. Nguyen had been caught with 4.2 kilograms of heroin—way above the 15 grams minimum that mandates the death penalty in Singapore. His days were numbered.

My interest in the death penalty and its abolition was no doubt inspired by the fact that I grew up just a few miles from a notorious British execution spot—Gallows Corner in Essex—where, in the eighteenth and nineteenth centuries, public hangings were a regular form of weekend entertainment just as the pubs opened. Of course, this was long before radio, movies, television and premier league football. There was little else to do and for many Britons this was a regular boozy carnival of the most appalling kind. Condemned prisoners were not always vicious criminals, or notorious masked and armed highwaymen such as the legendary Dick Turpin. Some were mere horse thieves, burglars or pickpockets, like 'Jenny Diver' of Mack the Knife notoriety, who took advantage of spectators at these spectacles and robbed them as the condemned swung from the gallows.

The original idea of having public executions in Britain was to frighten people to ensure they obeyed the law and would always be good, hard-working, upright, God-fearing citizens. It didn't seem to work, however. People still murdered, robbed, raped, burgled, stole sheep and horses, chopped down trees and picked pockets—all crimes that attracted the death penalty in those days. Much to the chagrin of many, public executions were banned in 1889, not only because they were suddenly deemed 'unseemly' or 'uncivilised' but also because the British establishment decided that putting people to death ought to be shrouded in mystery. Hangmen were made to sign the *Official Secrets Act*, forbidding them to talk or write about what they did and the horrors that inevitably took place. Until they became brave enough to defy it, newspaper editors came under the same act and faced fines and even jail. Arguments for and against capital punishment went on throughout the first half of the twentieth century, but in the aftermath of the Second World War there was a vociferous and powerful revival of the anti-hanging lobby.

In 1948, one of Britain's most ardent anti-death penalty campaigners, the Labour MP Sydney Silverman, said this in the House of Commons:

It is not only the melodrama and sensationalism with which these proceedings are surrounded, it is not only the sordid squalor, every detail of which spreads into newspapers in every one of these crimes, it is not only the relentless finality of this penalty. No one who knows the records can doubt that there have been cases of error, that there have been miscarriages of justice, and that innocent men have in fact been executed. Until human judgment is infallible, we have no right to inflict irrevocable doom. Above all these things, there is the sense which we all have that this penalty, of itself, denies the very principle on which we claim the right to inflict it—namely, the sanctity of human life. The sole justification, if there be one, for the retention of this penalty is that it is necessary to protect society. No one can prove that this is true, no one can prove that it is untrue, but we may compare it and draw inferences from the comparison with the state of affairs in other countries in which this penalty has been abolished.

In his reply, Conservative MP Sir David Maxwell Fyfe KC, who became Home Secretary in 1951, said he found it hard to accept the idea of judicial error:

Of course, a jury might go wrong, the Court of Appeal might go wrong, as might the House of Lords and the Home Secretary. They might all be stricken mad and go wrong. But that is not a possibility that anyone can consider likely. The honourable and learned Member is moving in a realm of fantasy when he makes that suggestion.

Nevertheless Silverman got his way by a large majority and the bill passed on to the House of Lords—where it was rejected, as expected, by a majority of 153. No executions were carried out while abolition was on the parliamentary agenda, and they were not resumed until November 1948, after a gap of nine months. The abolitionist movement grew stronger and resulted in a Royal Commission to examine capital punishment in all its distressing detail. The testimony of Albert Pierrepoint, Britain's most prolific executioner, who had practised his trade from the 1930s until his retirement in the 1950s, was instrumental in putting an end to the death penalty in Britain for good. The final victory came in 1965, just as Singapore gained its independence. By then, Darshan Singh was well into his career, executing people at the rate of about twelve a month.

The case for abolition of the death penalty is fairly compelling. Adam Hugo Bedau, a prominent member of the abolitionist movement in the United States, writes in *The Case against the Death Penalty*: 'A decent and humane society does not deliberately kill human beings. An execution is a dramatic, public spectacle of official, violent homicide that teaches the permissibility of killing people to solve social problems—the worst possible example to set for society.' And then there is perhaps the most fundamental argument against capital punishment—it is irreversible in cases of wrongful conviction.

Over the past three decades there has been a general trend towards abolition in most parts of the world. Today all European countries (with the exception of Belarus), most of Central and South America and about half of the African states have either made the death penalty illegal or it is effectively not in use. Amnesty International figures show that during the past decade, an average of over three countries a year have abolished the death penalty in law or, having done so for ordinary offences, have gone on to abolish it for all offences.

Of all the regions of the world it is Asia that has most resisted the abolitionist wave. From the Middle East to Japan judicial execution remains a fact of life and death, although Japan is at least beginning to debate its usefulness. But even here countries have not been entirely immune to abolition: in Southeast Asia, for example, Cambodia, the Philippines and Timor-Leste no longer provide for the death penalty for any crime.

There are now only fifty-eight countries that still use capital punishment. In these countries the death penalty is usually reserved as punishment for violent crimes such as rape or murder, but it may also be used to punish espionage, treason or mutiny, or sexual acts including adultery and sodomy. In China, serious cases of corruption may also be considered capital crimes.

But Singapore is in a class of its own, taking a morbid pride in the fact that it is known worldwide for the strictness of its laws. The *Misuse of Drugs Act* prescribes the death penalty for at least twenty drug-related crimes: possession of more than 500 grams of a 'soft' drug such as marijuana is punishable by death, and the same applies to hard drugs such as heroin or amphetamines in quantities of more than 15 grams. Those found guilty of gun crimes are also condemned to hang.

A UN study carried out in 2001 found that Singapore, per capita, had by far the highest execution rate in the world—three times higher than Saudi Arabia, the next highest. Its per capita prison population was extraordinarily high too—second only to the United States. The situation has not improved in the subsequent decade.

The basic argument in favour of capital punishment in Singapore—and everywhere else it is practised—is that it is a just and proper punishment for heinous offences and maintains law and order by deterring crime. Singapore's particular claim is that the death penalty is both necessary and effective in controlling the trade in illicit drugs, rampant in its region. (Singapore is neighbour to the so-called Golden Triangle, taking in Myanmar, Vietnam, Laos and Thailand—one of the world's largest opium-producing areas.) There was in fact an overall decline in the number of drug users arrested between 1994 and 2001, but since then drug abuse figures are on the rise again, particularly over the past four years—contradicting government claims that the threat of the death penalty is keeping Singapore safe from the scourge of drugs. Despite the harsh penalties for possession and trafficking, drug addiction remains a problem—particularly among marginalised groups including the poor and unemployed.

My own research confirms that justice in Singapore is patently biased against the weak and disadvantaged while favouring the wealthy and privileged. The death sentence is more likely to be imposed on those who are poorer and less educated. Other vulnerable groups include minorities and migrant workers. Reliance on the death penalty thus draws attention away from the true causes of crime, hindering social measures that might help control it.

In this book I expose many cases where young people in desperate situations have committed crimes after being seduced into acting as carriers for drug syndicates, then controlled through fear and threats of death. It is low-level mules, rather than the kingpins, who are most at risk of facing the gallows, and as long as this is the case, it is unlikely that capital punishment can truly have a deterrent effect.

Mr K. Shanmugam, now Singapore's Minister for Law and Minister for Home Affairs, told *Today*, a government-controlled free newspaper, that the death penalty for drug offences is a 'trade-off' the government must make to protect thousands of lives if drugs became freely available. He further explained that if Yong Vui Kong, a lowly mule on death row at the time of writing this edition, escaped the ultimate penalty, drug lords would see it as a sign that young traffickers will be spared and would then use more of them as drug mules. 'You save one life here, but ten other lives will be gone. What will your choice be?' he asked. Perhaps, I suggest, if anyone has to be hanged, more effort should be made to catch the syndicate bosses.

Singapore's use of the mandatory death penalty has attracted international criticism, particularly from Western nations and groups, but the government has vigorously defended its stance, arguing that the use of the death penalty is not a question of human rights, but one of an individual nation's freedom to make its own laws and enforce them as it sees fit.

This attitude was very apparent in the months leading up to the execution of convicted Australian drug trafficker, Nguyen Van Tuong, in December 2005. Singapore seemed determined not to give in to international pressure and to hang this young man come what may. As Singapore's publicity campaign went into higher gear,

Asad Latif, a former senior reporter with the *Straits Times*, and a visiting research fellow at the Institute of Southeast Asian Studies in Singapore, wrote:

> It is unfortunate Nguyen has to die, but the law against drug trafficking must be implemented uniformly. What is surprising, though, is how those aspects appear to have been subsumed by condemnations of an upstart city-state for having dared to condemn to death a citizen of an island-continent. They have the right, if they so wish, to argue that their laws are better than those of Singapore. But—and this is the critical caveat—no one has the right to expect, let alone demand, that Singapore bend its laws to suit the laws of another country.

Two days before the scheduled execution, Joseph K.H. Koh, the Singapore High Commissioner in Australia, wrote an article that was published in various Australian newspapers and on the internet. Capital punishment, he claimed, remains part of the criminal justice systems of seventy-six countries, including in the United States, where it is practised in thirty-eight states. 'We respect Australia's sovereign choice not to have capital punishment. We hope Australia will likewise respect Singapore's sovereign choice to impose the death penalty for the most serious crimes, including drug trafficking. The overwhelming majority of Singaporeans support this.'

Polls regularly indicate that a majority of Singaporeans support the death penalty, but Alex Au, an outspoken civil rights campaigner and death penalty abolitionist, disputes their findings. He maintains that for Singaporeans the subject of the death penalty is entirely off-limits. 'There is never any official discussion about it and no one really knows what happens when someone is hanged,' says Au. 'The subject of the death penalty is not even talked about on internet chatter which speaks to the nature of this society and how it sees—or doesn't see—the subject.'

Au is not the only one unhappy with the public silence on this issue. Tim Parritt, spokesman for the human rights watchdog Amnesty International, says: 'The concern Amnesty has about Singapore is the lack of information issued on executions, the number of executions and the processes which might feed a public debate and a higher level of public scrutiny about what is actually happening.'

Most executions in Singapore are carried out in complete secrecy and only occasionally acknowledged in the government-controlled media—except when a foreigner is involved. Apart from probing activists, only those officially in the know—the hangman, the prison governor, a doctor, a priest and a team of hopeful organ transplant surgeons—are aware that, on any given Friday, someone could be on their way to the gallows.

Singapore does not normally release statistics on the number of people it executes, but Amnesty International estimates that more than 400 were hanged from 1991 to 2001, mostly for drug trafficking and murder. In 2008 the figure could again only be guessed at—around 550. Only the government's well-guarded archives could reveal the actual figure but my own frequent requests and those of other interested parties have been ignored.

This might explain what I saw when I happened to switch on the television one afternoon in late September 2003. The then Singaporean Prime Minister, Goh Chok Tong, was being asked by BBC interviewer Tim Sebastian how many people had been executed so far that year. He looked surprised and said he 'believed' it was in the region of 'about seventy to eighty'. Asked why he did not know the precise number he replied curtly, 'I've got more important things to worry about.' Two days later his office issued a statement revising the figure down to ten. Not even the prime minister has these statistics readily to hand, it seems.

Singapore has also been strongly criticised by human rights groups which say its laws contains provisions that violate the right of presumption of innocence. The United Nations Special Rapporteur on Extra Judicial Summary and Arbitrary Executions, Philip Alston, has commented: 'It is a fundamental human right to be presumed innocent until proven guilty ... Singapore cannot reverse the burden and require a defendant to prove beyond reasonable doubt that he did not know he was carrying drugs'. Defendants in capital cases are not always given access to a lawyer until long after they have confessed to the police, sometimes following lengthy interrogations.

Alex Au says that there many areas in which Singapore's justice system is 'out of step with expected norms prevailing in many other countries', and that as a result, foreigners who tangle with the law in Singapore are often given special treatment. On his blog, Au has written that to foreigners—and many Singaporeans—Singapore's laws and processes appear 'barbaric and unjustifiably loaded against the accused'.

> Hence, each time a foreign government takes an interest in a case, we have to make ad hoc adjustments in order to avoid a crisis in relations ... But every time we make ad hoc adjustments we raise the question of equal justice. We raise the suspicion that the verdict might have been less grounded on facts than on diplomatic imperatives ...

No change is likely while the People's Action Party continues to dominate the political scene. Singapore's former prime minister and current 'minister mentor', Lee Kuan Yew, has made that clear. Lee is on record as having said that the basic difference in Singapore's approach springs from a traditional Asian value system that places the interests of the community over and above that of the individual. 'Our priority is the security and well-being of law-abiding citizens rather than the rights of the criminal to be protected from incriminating evidence.'

So I knew I was treading on dangerous ground when I embarked on an attempt to speak to Singapore's Chief Executioner and extract some of Singapore's most carefully guarded secrets from him. If I succeeded, it would make worldwide headlines. I also knew—and jokingly predicted at the time—I could end up in jail, and become a news item myself.

PART I

THE JOLLY HANGMAN

LOOKING FOR MR SINGH

I had no idea what to expect when I rang the doorbell. I was just hoping that this was the home of Darshan Singh and that he would kindly invite me in for a cup of tea and a chat and tell me some secrets he'd kept for close on half a century. More importantly, I wanted to talk to him about his next 'job': the execution of the Australian citizen Nguyen Van Tuong was only weeks or days away. Australia was slowly waking up to the fact that yet another of its citizens was about to be hanged in an Asian country for trafficking drugs.

I was on the tenth floor—or tenth drawer, a wag having once described Singapore's maze of uniform apartment blocks as being more like giant filing cabinets. I pressed the doorbell. It was 11.30 am. There was no sound from within. Ten, twenty seconds or so passed. I pressed again, this time a little more firmly. Then rustling sounds and muffled footsteps and the jangle of a bunch of keys came from within. I waited anxiously, holding my breath, wondering what kind of reception I would get if, indeed, this was the Chief Executioner's home. Many years earlier I had tried to interview Britain's last executioner, Harry Allen, who ran a pub near Manchester at a time when abolitionists were finally getting the upper hand. Change was coming, and Allen knew his days were numbered. Genial pub host though he was, he always refused to talk about his 'other job'. Hoping he would eventually change his mind, I would often call in for a pint and a chat whenever I passed by on my way to or from the *Daily Express* in Manchester where I was a staff reporter, but I never had any luck.

I was accompanied now by a young Singaporean photographer, Law Kian Yan, and I had prepared a little speech of introduction. Of course, I've never taken for granted what may happen in such situations. The worst experience during my long career as an investigative journalist was having a bucket of water thrown over my head from an upstairs window by a person of interest who did not want to talk to me. From then on I would always instinctively look up whenever I approached the front door of any potentially reticent interviewee.

In this case there was no window above the front door to worry about. But I wasn't at all sure I was standing on the right doorstep. I'd discovered that there were at least a dozen Darshan Singhs from one end of the island to the other. It would be like finding a Singh in Singapore! It had also occurred to me that none of the addresses I'd found were likely to be the home of the hangman, simply for security reasons. If I could find it, so could many others less well-intentioned. Being such a potentially vulnerable public servant, he might well have been provided with a government flat close to the prison and well protected by his armed colleagues on and off duty. There is always the risk of a grieving, maddened relative or friend exacting some form of retribution on hangmen. I recalled stories about British executioner Albert Pierrepoint having a police escort whenever he turned up at a prison to carry out his work. Sometimes he was armed with a hidden revolver in case things got out of hand, especially when he went to Germany to hang a Nazi war criminal. There were always angry scenes at the prison gates as campaigners gathered to protest the latest hanging.

So I was taking pot luck, really. I'd used my lucky number and stuck a proverbial pin in the seventh 'Darshan Singh' in the list, making the Woodlands address my first port of call. It was also the one closest to Bukit Timah, where I lived. All along I knew also that trying to interview Singapore's hangman could bring me into conflict with Singapore's *Official Secrets Act*.

Now I was praying that not only did I have the right man but also this one would be prepared to talk. Memories of Harry Allen's discreet silence did not help my confidence. I prayed a little harder. Kian Yan was holding a camera just below her waist. I'd instructed her that if Singh even opened the door and confirmed who he was to snatch a few shots. Then run! As we say in the newspaper business, a picture is worth a thousand words.

There was another jangle of keys as two locks clicked and the heavy, polished wooden door opened. A large stocky man appeared behind the wrought iron security gate. The first thing I noticed were his shining, dark eyes and large round face. He was nothing like I imagined an executioner to be. Wearing only a pair of baggy shorts and sandals, he seemed more like a kindly, if dishevelled, grandfather as he stood looking at me through the bars of the gate, a quizzical expression on his weathered face. I was not expecting him to look so ordinary, a person who would not necessarily stand out in a crowd, or someone you might see sitting quietly at a bar drinking a glass of beer.

'Yes?' he enquired.

'Excuse me,' I said. 'I'm looking for a Mr Darshan Singh ... but I'm not sure if I've come to the right address. Is your name Darshan Singh?'

'Yes.'

'There are at least a dozen Darshan Singhs in the records, so I might still have come to the wrong address. The gentleman I'm looking for used to be an officer at Changi Prison.'

'That's me,' he replied. 'I'm retired now.'

'But you still work there occasionally in another ... er ... capacity, don't you?' I added, affecting nervous hesitation, 'Er ... some ... er ... Friday mornings?'

A slight smile creased his weathered face. 'Yes.'

It made me feel more confident. 'A very special job, isn't it?'

'Yes.'

'And you have another very special job soon involving an Australian citizen?'

Given the history of the executions of Australians Kevin Barlow and Brian Chambers in Malaysia in July 1986, I knew Nguyen Van Tuong's execution could threaten a major diplomatic rift between Singapore and Australia. As I stood on the hangman's doorstep, time was running out for Nguyen. A frank interview with his executioner would be sensational—but getting an interview with the hangman at any time seemed like mission impossible. And I knew it would not please the powers that be in Singapore. 'He won't talk,' a local journalist friend had advised. 'Don't waste your time. And be careful. This is Singapore!'

But I was determined. It would not only make a good and timely story but also history. I'd be the first journalist to help break the *Official Secrets Act* concerning the death penalty. Capital punishment in the tiny island state had for far too long been shrouded in secrecy and discussion on the subject completely discouraged. It was time something was done about it. 'You could get two years behind bars,' my journalist friend had also warned. 'He might shop you to the authorities and have you arrested.'

I knew all that, but being trained in journalism in the old-fashioned 'publish and be damned' way of Fleet Street—once the newspaper capital of the world—I was determined to go ahead regardless. I did venture to enquire from an official at the Ministry for Home Affairs about the pending execution of Nguyen. The standard email response was always: 'We have a general policy not to give any information on the death penalty or the condemned.' So no one ever knows for sure who is about to be hanged or when. There are never angry, noisy protests outside Changi Prison like there used to be outside British prisons whenever an execution was about to take place. Such activism is severely discouraged in Singapore and the penalties for overstepping the mark can be dire. A gathering of more than four people to protest anything without permission can land the perpetrators in court, as many brave human rights activists have learned and are still learning.

I knew, of course, that an interview with this man would be bound to become a major topic of television and radio talk shows and help trigger a much wider anti-death penalty campaign around the world. In the eyes of many, including many Australians, Nguyen would finally cease to be just 'another Viet boy dealing smack'. It would also put the spotlight on Singapore's legal system, which many observers, inside and outside the country, believe has been perverted to suit political and economic expediency.

'Yes,' replied Singh, 'I will be hanging Nguyen Van Tuong very soon.'

His statement seemed to me to be a little premature. The President of Singapore had not even received a promised appeal from Australian Prime Minister John Howard in Canberra. Singh, it seemed, was certain Nguyen would not get a pardon. At least he was responding to my questions. But I still hadn't properly introduced myself.

'I'm a freelance journalist based here in Singapore,' I said. 'I would like to talk to you about Nguyen's execution.'

Singh smiled again and, without hesitation, unlocked the security gate and ushered us inside. 'Come in,' he said with a smile.

I shot a glance at Kian Yan as if to say, 'I can't believe this is happening ...' Not only had I found this needle in a haystack, he was prepared to talk—and with gracious hospitality!

'What would you like to drink?' he asked as we sat down.

He had a good selection of beers and I could see his drinks cabinet across the living room was well stocked with wine and spirits, including Chivas Regal, his favourite whiskey he told me later. I settled for a glass of Guinness and he disappeared to the kitchen. Several minutes later, as I sipped the perfectly chilled beer, a nagging feeling came over me: all this friendliness and hospitality might be too good to be true. Had he called the Internal Security Department or the prison governor? No sign of anything untoward at that moment! But a knock at the door or the blare of a police siren could still come at any time. I cast these thoughts to the back of my mind. The Guinness was going down nicely. They couldn't hang me, or even cane me for that, I joked to myself. But they could jail me for a few weeks or months or a year or so with a heavy fine. I knew that I should not be doing what I was doing. This was Singapore.

As we sat comfortably in armchairs opposite each other sipping drinks in his living room, Singh gave me a quizzical look. He wanted to know how I managed to find out who he was and where he lived.

'Finding your name was the hardest part,' I said. 'I found some public records but there were at least a dozen Darshan Singhs in the list. I chose the seventh on the list and decided to come here first.'

'Then this is your lucky day,' he said with a laugh.

It did not take much prompting for him to start going down memory lane. Born in 1933, he was an Indian Sikh and Muslim convert who grew up in Kuala Lumpur and first came to Singapore in 1957, after graduating from college. Malaya was in the last days of British rule and Singapore was not then separate and independent. The entire region was threatening more turmoil and it was still another eight years before complete independence finally came for the city-state.

Jobs were scarce amid the tension of Malaya's struggle for independence and the young Singh decided to travel south where opportunities were greater and the situation a little more promising. Looking through the jobs columns in the *Straits Times*, he saw an advertisement for young men and women to join the British Colonial Service and become officers in Changi Prison. He was accepted immediately and, after a short training course, was soon supervising dozens of prisoners on his block.

Capital punishment, of course, was a part of the colonial regime.

The chief hangman at that time was a Mr B. Seymour, whom Singh described as an 'English gentleman' and who was anxious to retire to become a partner in a chicken farm in Johor. So Seymour began looking around for an understudy to 'learn the ropes'. (This was one of Singh's jokes and he constantly peppered his conversation with his own personal brand of gallows humour, always breaking into guffaws of laughter as if he was hearing each one for the first time.)

Singh had just turned twenty-four and had a stout build and powerful arms. An impressive-looking young man who commanded authority, he seemed an obvious choice and, when approached by Seymour to see if he would like to take over his job and hang people, he agreed without hesitation. It also meant extra money. Bonuses were paid on a per head basis. Each hanging brought in around $30 in those days.

When Singh became Chief Executioner in 1959 he was one of the highest paid prison officers. Business on the gallows was brisk. He was only twenty-six and had just married a Muslim woman slightly younger than himself. She had no idea what his other duties were inside Changi, other than that he was a prison officer. He had, after all, signed the *Official Secrets Act* and did not feel guilty about not telling her. He could tell no one he was Chief Executioner. But his wife finally discovered that whenever he left home on a Friday at around 2.30 am it was to hang someone. Horrified, she left him. Singh refused to discuss that episode in his life, but I learned from another source that she was appalled that her young husband killed people on behalf of the State.

Darshan Singh himself firmly believes he was doing an important job in the service of Singapore. As we sat and talked, he reminisced about his grim calling with surprising frankness, as though he had been waiting a long time and was anxious for recognition. And he emphasised that he had no regrets about his work at the gallows, a career few would even dream of following. 'I was just doing my job, lah', he said many times. 'It was an important job.'

Dangerous criminals have to be removed from society never to be given a chance to commit abominable crimes again, he said. Everyone knows the harsh laws of Singapore which began under British colonial rule, and if they commit the crime they must do the time—either behind bars or on the end of the rope. This attitude extends to the many condemned who have come his way—especially drug traffickers, child killers, rapists, brutal murderers and armed robbers.

The father of three adopted children and now a grandfather, Singh told me he would always support the death penalty in his country. 'It has helped keep Singapore one of the safest places on earth,' he often told me. 'These drug traffickers know what will happen to them if they get caught. People who sympathise with them have nothing to say about the thousands who suffer because of drugs. They destroy their lives as well as their families—and society as a whole suffers.' He believes it was a big mistake for countries such as Britain and Australia to abolish the death penalty. 'I have read that some people in England—and also in Australia—would like capital punishment to be brought back. If they do and they ever need a hangman again, I would offer my services,' he told me during one of the several interviews I had with him. He revealed that he once travelled secretly to Calcutta, India, to carry out the hanging of a rapist. 'I don't often get these requests,' he told me, but said he was always at the service of any government anywhere to carry out an execution by hanging. 'If the condemned man or woman has been properly tried in court I would do it without hesitation.'

2

THE ISLE OF EASE UPRISING

If Darshan Singh ever doubted his abilities when it came to getting the calculations right for a perfect hanging, all that changed at dawn one Friday morning in 1964 when he began executing eighteen men, three at a time. He knew he was going to have a major job on his hands when he began reading the trial of fifty-eight convicts who had been charged with the murder of the British superintendent and two deputies of an experimental penal colony on Pulau Senang—or Isle of Ease—just 10 miles south of Singapore. But he had no idea just how many would actually be sentenced to death. The bets were on that only six would hang and the rest receive varying prison sentences or be acquitted. He had been Chief Executioner for four years, and six hangings in a day would have been a record and a major task for him then, the gallows being equipped to hang only three at one time. Eighteen executions to be completed in one day in six separate batches was more than a challenge.

The tiny island had been chosen by the not then fully independent Singapore to keep violent, dangerous criminals in isolation from the general population. It was believed such men could be reformed and turned into good citizens. The government chose an idealistic British prison officer, Daniel Stanley Dutton, as the perfect man to run the place. He would supervise the building of the settlement and teach the inmates pride and self-reliance. Although a strict disciplinarian who believed in hard work to keep prisoners' minds off other things, he also believed that if you treated men like these with respect and in a civilised but disciplined way, they would reform and become good, productive citizens after their release. Dutton, who had seen active service in the British Army when he parachuted into German-occupied Greece during the Second World War and later in Palestine, spurned armed guards to protect him and his small staff from potential violence and refused any kind of personal weapons.

The tropical island was deceptive in name as well as appearance. The new arrivals found they had to carve a settlement out of virgin jungle to make it habitable for themselves and their overseers. The sparkling blue waters surrounding the 202-acre island were home to vicious man-eating sharks, powerful currents and treacherous hidden coral reefs which were thought sufficient deterrent to make any detainee think twice before attempting to escape. Apart from 277 officially counted coconut trees, everything else that swayed was formidable jungle. If all this was not depressing enough for the new inhabitants, the island had a long, gloomy history, a past they soon learned about and tagged on to. According to legend, the original inhabitants became victims of the curse of a thirsty old man. One day long, long ago, the old man went looking for a drink of water. But the islanders, always in fear of their two meagre streams running dry, refused to give him any. So the old man put a curse on them and while the tiny streams continued to flow, the original inhabitants mysteriously disappeared one by one.

The modern history of the island is equally bleak. When the first survey was made in January 1960 the island's population totalled two: Adolf Monteiro, a one-time keeper of Raffles Lighthouse, and his son, Steven. The Monteiros had moved to the deserted island in 1937 to run a tiny copra industry. Monteiro and his son remained during the Japanese occupation, but although they were left alone, they witnessed the brutal treatment of labour gangs forced to grow tapioca and other crops. Through disease, hunger and ill-treatment the labourers too died one by one. All over the island shallow graves of those men can still be found. But the Isle of Ease's gloomy history was about to get gloomier still—and Chief Executioner Singh would become an important part of that particular story.

The first escape bid was staged in January 1961, when three detainees vanished into the jungle. They were back only days later, exhausted and hungry with thoughts of freedom far from their minds. As time passed, the escape attempts became a little more sophisticated, more daring, but just as futile. The most dramatic occurred in December 1962 when five prisoners seized a powerful military speedboat and raced to find cover on one of Indonesia's thousands of islands. A customs boat intercepted and rammed the fleeing speedboat, throwing the occupants into the shark-infested waters. Luckily for them they were not eaten alive.

The first indication of any large-scale revolt came in early 1963 when fourteen inmates armed with *changkol* (hoes) attacked a settlement assistant and then fled into the jungle only to be recaptured a few days later. While an inquiry was still pending, an even bigger revolt was being hatched. It came suddenly and brutally on the morning of 12 July 1963, at a time when the penal camp experiment had appeared in some ways to be a success story. The most heart-warming piece of news was that a detainee had passed his higher school certificate examination. Dutton, who regarded the settlement as his baby, was extremely proud of this achievement.

Major Peter James, a retired regular British Army officer, then Director of Singapore Prisons, arrived at his office in Upper Pickering Street just before lunchtime after an inspection tour of Changi Prison. A radio message had just come in from Dutton giving news of a rumour that trouble was brewing—with the ominous threat that 'they are out to get me'. The two then argued about what to do next. Dutton said he had arrested the ringleaders and had everything under control. Despite Dutton's protests, James contacted the Deputy Commissioner of Police, Cheah Teng Check, who immediately ordered a troop unit to the island. With them went officers from Changi Prison—including Darshan Singh—armed only with heavy batons to quell the riot. But by the time these men were despatched, the situation was completely out of control. Frantic calls were then heard over the radio transmitter. It was Dutton calling for help. 'Situation very bad,' he kept repeating, until the radio room was in flames and he lay dying.

When the police arrived on the island all was quiet. None of the prisoners offered any resistance. Some were even seen playing guitars and singing songs, according to court records. After an investigation fifty-eight were charged with rioting and the murders of Dutton and his assistants, Arumugam Veerasingham and Tan Kok Hian. The prisoners were mostly hardened criminals or secret society members detained without trial and, despite Dutton's promises, many had little or no hope of ever leaving the island. They complained of being over-worked like slaves, often late into the night. Allegations of corruption were rife; it was claimed that in return for bribes some prisoners were given preferential treatment and allowed to return to the mainland at weekends for family visits in Changi Prison. While this was found to be untrue, the rumours persisted. Prisoners also felt the system of release was biased and unpredictable. Dutton's faith in this brave new world had come to a violent end.

It was to be a significant trial, reported in the *Malayan Law Journal* as being unparalleled in the legal history of Singapore and Malaya. A special dock had to be built in the Assize Court to accommodate all the accused, and ensuring everyone had a fair hearing was an enormous task. The trial was to last an unprecedented sixty-four days. Singh helped escort the prisoners back and forth every day for the trial and formed part of the guard inside the court room, he told me during one of several interviews. A seven-member jury of Singaporean civilians—Chinese, Malay and Indian—would decide the fate of the convicted. The evidence they were to hear was lurid in the extreme. One archived newspaper report in the *Straits Times* quoted detainee and chief prosecution witness, Liew Woon, who said he saw Dutton 'being burned alive and assaulted with an axe' by two armed rioters. Liew said two other detainees—Sim Hoe Seng, who was carrying a tin of petrol, and Chan Wah, who had the axe—climbed onto the roof of the settlement's radio room. He said Chan smashed the wooden roof and Sim set the building ablaze. Liew said Dutton—'with part of his body on fire'—tried to escape but was confronted by four other accused, one of whom slashed him with a *parang* (machete) and another with an axe before he collapsed.

With such sensational revelations, the court reports made compulsive reading in newspapers all over Malaya, in Singapore's *Straits Times* and back in Britain. Readers followed the grim details that were published under such headlines as 'Dutton Was In Flames When He Was Cut Down'. At the trial the Public Prosecutor, Francis T. Seow, said Dutton had died a terrible death having 'blundered' by underestimating the strength of the uprising; Seow claimed a 'quite sizeable section' of the 316 detainees on the island that day were involved in the rioting.

As Chief Executioner, Singh was in a unique position, being able to follow the trial both in court and in the *Straits Times*. Then aged thirty, he was quite experienced in the job, but still he did not know exactly how many he would be obliged to hang. Most observers guessed that only the ringleaders would get the death sentence. So it came as a surprise to everyone—especially to Singh—when he heard Mr Justice Buttrose deliver the sentences. The news to the general public came on the morning of Friday, 13 March 1964, when the front-page headline in the *Straits Times* screamed: 'Senang Revolt: 18 To Hang'.

Although he would be provided with a team of assistants to control the men, shackle arms behind backs and legs together, then help lead them to the gallows, it was still an awesome responsibility. He must carry out the executions as quickly and humanely as possible.

The eighteen were separated in individual cells that Friday morning in 1964. A guard stood at each cell door. Each prisoner had already been weighed and measured. They were of varying weight, height and muscularity and Singh had to ensure he got his sums exactly right. He did not want anything to go wrong. 'If you get it wrong the head would go one way and the body the other,' he told me.

Singh had been taught the so-called Table of Drops by Seymour, the last British colonial hangman. He quipped more than once that he'd been quick to 'learn the ropes'. It was a system devised by the nineteenth-century cobbler-turned-hangman, William Marwood. Each prisoner is dropped an exact length according to their weight and height, modified if required to take account of their physique and muscularity, especially the neck. The force of the drop combined with the position of the knot below the left ear is designed to cause instant unconsciousness, then rapid death. The prisoner is weighed prior to execution and the weight in pounds—less an allowance of 14 pounds for the head—divided into 1020 to arrive at a drop in feet. It takes between half and three-quarters of a second for the prisoner to reach the bottom of the drop, once the trap is sprung. A heavy person would require a short drop and a light person a longer drop. The Table of Drops, Singh insists, is the most 'humane' method of hanging, as it prevents slow strangulation or decapitation—provided that the calculations are correct.

This would be one of the biggest tests of his career. As the new day began, helped by two assistants per prisoner, he led them in single file three at a time into the execution chamber, their arms already secured tightly behind their backs. They were then made to stand on the twin trap doors, where their legs were strapped together. Any last minute struggling and kicking out as they plunged downwards when the trap doors opened might mean starting all over again. It was a spectacle none of the witnesses—the prison governor, doctor and other officials—wanted to see twice. It was nightmarish enough, even with their experience.

The prisoners died together three at a time but not before their executioner uttered what he thought were comforting words: 'I am sending you to a better place than this.' According to policy the bodies had to remain hanging for ten to twenty minutes to ensure death had taken place, or until the prison doctor certified such. Those waiting for their turn could hear the clunk of the trap doors as they simultaneously opened and three dull thuds. They were already helpless with their arms pinioned behind their backs. Panic set in for many and they began wailing in terror.

It was important to get it all over with as quickly as possible. Each batch took almost 40 minutes from the time the prisoners were prepared, put on the gallows, then left to hang for the prescribed time. The bodies were removed as soon as they were pronounced dead by the prison doctor. The gallows then had to be checked to ensure the mechanism would work the next time. Even so, they were being executed at a fast rate and the entire gruesome process was all over well before lunchtime. Nothing had gone wrong. The eighteen corpses were lined up in the prison morgue awaiting disposal. The unclaimed bodies were sent to a crematorium chosen by the prison; the others were taken by grieving relatives for funeral services according to their religion.

Singh had undertaken the most arduous and macabre task of his career. Perhaps it was the largest of its kind in the life of any executioner in history. The men he hanged were: Tan Kheng Ann, alias Robert Black, alias Ang Chua; Chia Yeow Fatt, alias Botak; Cheong Wai Sang, alias Genii; Subramaniam Somasundram; Bobby Lim Tee Kang; Vengadasalam Somasundarjoo; Lim Kim Chuan, alias Tua Tai; Khoo Geok San, alias Kapalu Batu; Chan Wah; Hoe Hock Hai; Govindasamy Ponnapalam; Chew Seng Hoe; Chew Thiam Huat, alias Baby Chai; Sim Hoe Seng; Ng Cheng Liong; Tan Yin Chwee; Sim Teck Beng; and Cheng Poh Kheng.

But the ordeal was not over for all those who helped send the eighteen convicted killers to their deaths or put the others behind bars for many years. It was feared that the prosecution team and

Judge Buttrose himself would now be targeted by secret societies out to get revenge. Buttrose was guarded round the clock until he was repatriated to Britain. Although Francis T. Seow, Senior Crown Counsel, and his assistant K.S. Rajah, Director of Public Prosecution, were also given police protection until it was deemed that any possible threat to their lives no longer existed, Singh said he was never given any protection himself. Perhaps the authorities thought he was safe working in Changi Prison surrounded by armed fellow officers. But in fact that could have been the most dangerous place for the hangman to be at that time—surrounded also by vicious criminals out for revenge.

3

GALLOWS HUMOUR

If Darshan Singh has a macabre sense of humour it should surprise no one. Making jokes in the face of nightmarish situations is a part of human nature, an inborn defence mechanism, psychologists will tell you. The hangman's lot cannot be a happy one. Unless, of course, he is heartless, sadistic and really enjoys what he does. Even if they have such perverted natures—as perverted perhaps as some of those they execute—it must be a heavy burden to bear, despite any outward show of bravado and self-righteousness. Although he would not admit it, Singh's burden must be particularly heavy.

To understand the weight of this burden, it is important to know what happens before and after anyone is hanged. Singh himself has a special way of helping some of the death row inmates he has known come to terms with their fate. He always talks quietly and explains the process as kindly as possible. He promises they will feel no pain, that he is an expert with many years' experience. He told me he so convinced the eighteen men convicted of murder arising from the Pulau Senang 'Isle of Ease' penal colony riots of 1963 that being hanged by him would be painless and all over in a split-second, that they wanted only him to hang them.

Singh proudly declared to me that, with his long experience, he could ensure a condemned man or woman was always hanged quickly, efficiently and painlessly. 'An inexperienced hangman could make mistakes and prolong suffering,' he explained. 'They don't struggle when I hang them. I know the correct way it should be done. With an inexperienced executioner, who doesn't know what he is doing, they will struggle like chickens, like fish out of the water.'

On occasions when an executioner is not sure if a prisoner will fight on the way to the gallows, a prison doctor prescribes a relaxant to help him—or her—stay as calm as possible. The drug is usually slipped into a last drink the night before. But there is very little chance of anything really violent happening, Singh told me. An assistant or guard usually stands by while preparations are completed. The prisoners' arms are quickly pinioned behind their backs with handcuffs and straps, rendering them virtually helpless. Aided by an assistant, Singh hastens them into the execution chamber via a connecting door and before they know what is happening, the noose is in position.

In true Singaporean tradition timing also has to be perfect. Why hangings are carried out just as the sun rises has never been clearly explained to me. Perhaps it is to do with the date on which the execution has been ordered—to ensure the condemned will never see the light of another day or even a fraction of one beyond his or her legally determined lifespan.

As the body hangs suspended for the requisite time, underneath the cloth hood the face will be purple, engorged with blood, the neck covered with lacerations, the tongue swollen and protruding from the mouth, eyes bulging. And involuntary ejections of urine and faeces stain the deceased's clothing.

Singh admitted that the most difficult part of his job was when he had to hang prisoners whom he had befriended. Getting to know some prisoners languishing on death row, he said he developed close relationships with them while still eventually having to carry out the execution.

'In a way, I became their friend and they wanted only me to hang them when they finally accepted their fate. They trusted me that they would feel no pain. One of the fellows even asked me to give him his final haircut the day before.'

Singh told me that he wanted to retire one day but the authorities could not find a replacement hangman. Not long ago he spent weeks training two understudies, one Chinese and the other Malay. Using dummies he taught them how to calculate the length of rope required. He told them it was important to get the drop exactly right. Too short and they are strangled. Too long and they are decapitated, he always reminded them. And before the short walk to the scaffold, the arms must be pinioned behind backs, the nooses placed around the necks, the white caps on heads. Singh even told the trainees that he always uttered the same words: 'I am sending you to a better place than this.' Perhaps he wanted them to carry on the tradition that he began. But when it came to a real execution, the would-be executioners froze. They could not pull the lever. According to Singh, the young Chinese prison officer actually ran from the execution chamber in horror. He resigned from the prison service the next day. The Malay prison officer returned to his normal duties but refused to go anywhere near the scaffold again. Singh was obliged to stick at the job while more attempts were made to find his successor.

During conversations I had with him, I asked Singh if he experienced nightmares. Did he ever see the faces of any of those whose lives he has snuffed out mocking him during a disturbing dream? I almost believed him when he said he always sleeps well and what he does has never bothered him or disturbed his peace of mind ... until he began reeling off jokes and laughing heartily. 'After every execution,' he says, 'it takes me two days to get over my hangover.' The conversation continues. Another joke. More hearty laughter. 'I am the fastest executioner in the world,' he says. 'I don't hang about.'

Singh has kept his sanity about his work and lightens his load by repeating his half dozen or so jokes, conversational set pieces he recounts at the dinner table or over a glass of beer in one of his favourite haunts in Singapore's Little India. He even told me about a certain execution many years ago that was celebrated with two fellow prison officers. It was the evening after his 500th execution. The officers came to his home in civilian clothes with a bottle or two of Chivas Regal. 'I can't remember whose execution we were celebrating, who the 500th person was,' he said. 'It was a long time ago ...'

Sigmund Freud had a theory about gallows humour. In his 1927 essay 'Der Humor', he wrote: 'The ego refuses to be distressed by the provocations of reality, to let it be compelled to suffer. It insists that it cannot be affected by the traumas of the external world; it shows, in fact, that such traumas are no more than occasions for it to gain pleasure.'

Listening to Singh reminisce and make decidedly off-colour jokes reminded me of the Hungarian-born author Arthur Koestler, who played a crucial part in the campaign to abolish capital punishment in Britain back in the 1950s. In his damning *Reflections on Hanging*, which was serialised in British Sunday newspaper the *Observer*, Koestler opened with a startling reference to Britain as a 'peaceful country where necks are broken', and commented:

> There seems to be jolliness about the procedure as if the victim, twitching on the end of the rope, was not a real person but a dummy burnt on Guy Fawkes' Day. The present hangman, Albert Pierrepoint, runs a public house called Help the Poor Struggler ... and the present Lord Chief Justice delighted a Royal Academy banquet with a story of a judge who, after passing the death sentence on three men, was welcomed by a band playing the Eton Boating Song's refrain: 'We'll all swing together' ... It all goes to show that hanging has a kind of macabre cosiness, like a slightly off-colour family joke, which only foreigners, abolitionists and other humourless creatures are unable to share.

At one time the prison authorities considered abandoning hanging, and replacing it with the lethal injection method used in some

American states. Two arguments quickly put paid to that idea.

One was the tradition in Changi Prison for the condemned to be given the opportunity to agree to organ donation. Singh revealed to me that one of his duties was to try to persuade the men and women he was about to hang to sign a consent form giving permission to the authorities to donate their organs. Many agreed, while others recoiled in horror at the thought that their bodies would be 'butchered' in this way. Murderers and drug traffickers deserve their fate, Singh believes, and their punishment is a means of 'complete rehabilitation', but he also believes in reincarnation and would tell the men and women he was obliged to hang that if they repented and did something good before they died they would return as better men or women when they were 'reborn'.

I found out through another source that anyone who signs the consent form to donate their organs for transplant or research is put on a special regime. Known as the Death Row Diet, this consists of fresh fish, beef, chicken, lamb, and a wide variety of fruit, nuts and vegetables, chocolate, sweets, biscuits and fruit juices. 'They are given any high-quality, nutritious food they want,' said my contact, a lawyer who was involved in trying to save one of these youngsters. 'The idea is to ensure their organs are in perfect condition for transplant after they are hanged. They are given huge portions of anything they want. But first they must sign a consent form to qualify for this special treatment to be fed like battery hens before they are slaughtered. If they refuse, they get normal prison food.'

Beyond the walls of Changi Prison hanged prisoners' organs are worth tens of thousands of dollars each. Wealthy medical tourists are prepared to pay huge sums for a kidney, heart or liver transplant. I was also told that some would-be recipients living overseas are summoned to Singapore—after blood-matching tests are complete— just before an execution is due to be carried out. 'It's important that transplants are carried out as soon as possible after death,' the lawyer told me. 'The fresher they are the better.'

But these lucky ones would never know if their lives had been saved by someone who had just been hanged. Susan Ho, whose title is 'business office leader' at Singapore General Hospital, which provides medical services for locals and foreigners alike, told me they see many desperate patients from overseas. Medical tourism is big business in the Lion City with many patients flying in from other Southeast Asian countries, the US, Europe and Japan. She says they never know the names of the donors and would have no idea if any organ had been harvested in Changi Prison's execution chamber. 'This kind of information is confidential to the recipient,' she said. 'We do not know who the donors are. Many may be the result of traffic accidents.'

Fees charged by Singapore General range from S$133,940 to S$167,165—and that's only for the ward and surgical procedure, Susan Ho told me during a telephone conversation, believing I was a friend of a wealthy foreigner dying for want of a kidney transplant. The cost of a kidney, liver or heart was not included, she said, adding that she could not tell me how much any of these organs might cost. That was a confidential matter.

So it seems the sky's the limit when someone else's life is at risk on death row. In September 2008, Singapore retail magnate Tang Wee Sung was fined $17,000 and sentenced to one day in jail for agreeing to purchase a single kidney for $300,000 from two middle men and lying about its source—a poverty-stricken Indonesian man struggling to feed his family. But Tang got a new kidney after all—donated by gangster Tan Chor Jin, who was hanged in Changi Prison on the morning of 9 January 2009, for shooting a nightclub owner to death. It was said at his trial that Tan entered Lim Hock Soon's flat on the morning of 15 February 2006, and ordered him to tie up his wife, daughter and their maid. Tan fired six rounds from a pistol, hitting Lim five times and killing him instantly. Known as the 'One-eyed Dragon' because he was blind in one eye, Tan was arrested in a hotel raid by Malaysian police after he fled to Kuala Lumpur. Tang received

Tan's kidney in the National University Hospital later on the day of Tan's execution. The *Straits Times* and the *New Paper* reported in the days before Tan's execution that he had told his wife and mistress he wanted to donate his organs after his death.

Now, in a bid to alleviate a worldwide shortage of organs, the Singapore government is considering legalising the trade with live donors—inspired perhaps by the case of Tang, which revealed its enormous money-making and life-saving potential. But inside modern Changi Prison organ donation is already legal provided the consent forms are in order. Death row holds 'Cluster A' prisoners and the cells and gallows have been specially built close to the prison hospital. No time is wasted. Listening to my informant it all seemed like something that could only have come from the imaginings of Aldous Huxley in his futuristic fiction, *Brave New World*. Organ harvesting has to be a clinically well-organised procedure. As soon as the condemned prisoners sign the consent form, blood samples are taken to match with potential recipients. The organs most in demand are hearts, kidneys, livers, lungs, pancreases, intestines and corneas, but blood and all kinds of body tissue including skin and skeletal frames are also frozen or preserved in special solutions for research or life-saving procedures.

The Medical Singapore website boasts that because most of Singapore's doctors and surgeons have been educated in Western countries, they have the experience and expertise to offer world-class care, while 'representing considerable cost savings in comparison to the United States and Europe'. But would cashed-up medical tourists prefer to go elsewhere if they knew their freshly harvested organ had been donated by a young man or woman whose life had just been snuffed out on the gallows?

So, that was the first argument against lethal injection: the prisoner's vital organs would be destroyed and could not be donated. But I believe the second argument, though simpler, was even more important. The proposal was shelved because it removed key elements of being executed on the gallows: the stark fear and horror; the utter ignominy of being hanged by your fellow countrymen. Lethal injection, to the Singaporean way of thinking, is too humane, too painless and too dignified. It would be more like lying on a gurney ready for surgery and never waking up from the anaesthetic.

It is the very dread of being hanged and the awful spectre of the gallows, death penalty advocates maintain, that is so important. Hanging is the ultimate degradation.

4

A TALE OF TWO HANGMEN

When I asked Darshan Singh exactly how many he had executed, he thought for a moment. 'Not really sure, lah,' he said. 'Can be over 1000, can be under.'

He once hoped that his name would some day appear in the *Guinness Book of Records* as the most prolific executioner of all time—with special mention of what he regards as his greatest accomplishment: the day he hanged those eighteen men from the Isle of Ease whose trial and conviction for murder he had witnessed from start to finish. He told me that he had actually applied to the publishers for this recognition, but when I enquired at their offices in London I was told his request had been denied. No reason was given. Perhaps such a record was considered too unsavoury for this revered and popular family publication. Or maybe Singh had to do the impossible—provide proof, something the Singapore government would never allow.

I tried contacting the Ministry for Home Affairs myself, but they could not verify the figure Singh had quoted me. For the government, anything to do with the death penalty must always be shrouded in mystery. No official statistics have ever been made available—but if Singh's estimate is accurate, it defies belief.

The previous 'record holder' was Englishman Albert Pierrepoint, who carried out executions in prisons all over Britain and in occupied Germany. Some of those he hanged were Second World War Nazi criminals and spies. Pierrepoint began his career in the 1930s, following in the footsteps of his uncle, Thomas Pierrepoint, and his father, Henry Pierrepoint. For more than half a century the Pierrepoints dominated the list of official executioners in Britain. But the total number they hanged comes nowhere near Singh's astonishing claim. When he retired in 1956 Albert Pierrepoint's 'kills' totalled 435—less than half of Singh's personal tally. What's more, Singapore's population was a mere two million in 1959 when Singh took on the job. Even now it is still just nudging five million. The UK population, in contrast, was around 48 million when Albert Pierrepoint began his career in the 1930s. It's not surprising the Singapore government is reluctant to keep an official tally of deaths by hanging; the statistics would surely reveal that the Lion City has one of the highest per capita execution rates in the world.

Like Singh, Albert Pierrepoint was proud of what he had done on behalf of the state and kept detailed records of those he hanged. He believed he was put on earth especially to do the work he did and was 'protected by a higher power' throughout his long career. 'It is no source of pride, it is simply history, that I have carried out the execution of more judicial sentences of death than any executioner in any British record or archive,' he said. But then he added: 'That fact is the measure of my experience. The fruit of my experience has this bitter after-taste: that I do not now believe that any one of the hundreds of executions I carried out has in any way acted as a deterrent against future murder. Capital punishment, in my view, achieved nothing except revenge.'

Singh spoke to me in similar if less grandiose terms. But far from considering what he did was a waste of time, he sincerely believes he has helped make Singapore an ideal place for its citizens to live in peace and harmony and the economic success that it is today. Whether or not he will one day come to the same conclusion as Pierrepoint and condemn his life's work is something only he can decide. Looking at those smiling, shiny dark eyes as we talked it was impossible to detect what was really going on in his mind. But I sometimes suspect that he had his own demons to deal with in the middle of the night.

In 1965, when the death penalty was finally abolished in Britain for all time, it was in large part due to Albert Pierrepoint's boldness when he and some British newspapers first broke the *Official Secrets Act*. He was not prosecuted; no doubt it was considered that much worse would have come out at his trial. Nonetheless, Pierrepoint's daring—albeit for money and publicity to boost the takings at his pub—had a huge effect on the public conscience and the eventual decision to do away with the gallows forever.

When Singh innocently broke Singapore's very own *Official Secrets Act* by allowing me to interview him—which made waves around the world—the establishment no doubt became fearful that their own citizens might one day catch the abolitionist bug. Not a word of the interview was published in any of the government-controlled newspapers, including the *Straits Times*. Only the *New Paper* published a report on its front and inside pages—and that was an attack on me for allegedly 'tricking' Singh into spilling the beans and embarrassing Singapore. Those were not Singh's words but the words of the *New Paper*.

I am told, however, that the shock waves that went through the halls of the Presidential Palace when my interview was first published in the *Australian*, a national Australian daily and one of that country's biggest newspapers, were palpable. It was the kind of publicity Singapore dreads. For the authorities it was a major loss of face. Anti-death penalty activists everywhere condemned Singapore—'a nation with ice in its veins'—without mercy. It was the very stuff that so alarmed the British establishment back in the 1940s and 1950s when abolitionists, empowered by evidence that innocent men had been hanged, finally claimed the moral high ground. Singapore was now getting the same kind of treatment and didn't like it one bit.

PART II

SINGAPORE JUSTICE IN THE DOCK

5

MAN IN TRANSIT

The neatly dressed young man strolled nonchalantly through Terminal One's transit lounge at Changi Airport, trying to look every bit a typical student traveller without a care in the world. He was returning from a trip to Phnom Penh, Cambodia, and looking forward to being home with his family in Melbourne for the Christmas holiday. But his cool look belied what was really going on behind that inscrutable face. It was 12 December 2002, a date he would come to remember until the end of his days. There would not be many more of them. Although he didn't know it then, there were only another 1085 days left. The countdown had begun for Australian citizen, Nguyen Van Tuong.

Completely in the dark as to the nature of her son's trip, Kim Nguyen, a devout Catholic, was at home busily preparing for the Christmas celebrations and a welcome meal for Nguyen. She expected him to walk through the door at breakfast time. But it was a meal he would never eat and a welcome he would never receive.

The twenty-two-year-old was particularly looking forward to seeing his twin brother, Khoa. He had a very special Christmas present for him. It was strapped to his back and hidden in his luggage. Silk Air Flight MI622 from Phnom Penh touched down at Terminal One at precisely 3.06 pm. The connecting flight that would take Nguyen home on the final leg of the journey was Qantas Airways QF10. He had quite a long wait. Take-off time was not until 8.15 pm. Nguyen tried to remain composed as possible, anxious not to make eye contact with anyone. He held on tightly to his canvas bag. The haversack slung over his left shoulder was secure beneath his arm. He looked around for a quiet spot to spend the next five hours. He wanted to look natural but his stomach was churning and deep down he was feeling extremely nervous. He purchased a magazine and many cups of coffee and tried to take the nagging fear off his mind. Nguyen kept glancing at the brand new $1000 Rado wristwatch he had bought himself for his twenty-first birthday, hoping his nervousness was not being noticed. He knew hidden CCTV cameras were quietly whirring away and men and women trained in reading body language would be sitting at batteries of screens looking for telltale signs of trouble or anxious people with something to hide or fear. Terrorists were their priority targets. And drug traffickers. Security officers in uniform and some in plain clothes pretending to be fellow travellers were everywhere, ready to respond to any eventuality. Nguyen was also aware that other eyes could be watching him. The syndicate in Phnom Penh had warned he would be shadowed every step of the way to make sure he delivered. Even if they were bluffing, he would take no chances. The man in the seat behind him might have been one of them. Any deviation, change of heart, would mean serious trouble. He feared for his life from all quarters. He just wanted to get home, safe and sound, be among family and friends again. Just after 7.15 pm he heard the Qantas flight announcement. He downed the last dregs of the coffee to keep his mouth from drying up, gathered his belongings and began walking slowly towards Gate C22.

Nguyen knew the next few steps would be the most hazardous part of the journey. His very life was on the line. He understood the meaning of those four simple words, always in English, on the sign he had just passed: 'Death To Drug Traffickers.' They were everywhere—on immigration and customs declaration forms and walls at every checkpoint. Nguyen did his best to maintain an impassive look as he was motioned through the arch of the metal detector by a female security officer. The canvas bag and haversack were going through the x-ray machine to his left. His heart almost missed a beat as the alarm sounded. But this was not unusual. A bunch of keys, a belt buckle, a mobile phone or a few coins could do that. He stayed cool—on the outside. The officer told him to stand facing her, legs apart on two 'Big Foot' imprints embedded in the thick carpet. She passed a hand-held metal detector around his body, front and back, up and down and between his legs. No alarm this time. Nguyen breathed a sigh of relief. But it was not over yet. The officer then ran her hand gently over Nguyen's back. Perhaps she had already sensed there was something suspicious under his jacket. Or perhaps she already knew more than he imagined. Perhaps she had been waiting for him. Whatever the reason, she called a male officer to take a closer look, a closer feel.

He was taken to a room for a more intrusive search. His haversack and canvas bag were now being carried by the officer. His heart was pounding. Inside the search room, Nguyen was ordered to take off his jacket and shirt. He did as he was told without further prompting. Then he turned around. A plastic packet was strapped to his lower back with yellow and white adhesive tape. He also had half a dozen counterfeit watches and a number of belts—Christmas presents for friends—in the haversack with a second plain packet. At this point the police officer called for his superior, Sergeant Teh Kim Leng, to take over the questioning. Nguyen's calm demeanour turned to sheer terror. Streaks of sweat ran down his forehead. He cried, banged his head against the wall, and crumpled to the floor, howling, rocking back and forth with his head in his hands. He would never see his family and friends in Melbourne again. He would now be rerouted. Destination: Changi Prison.

The questioning began. 'What's this on your back?'

'Heroin.'

'What's inside the haversack?'

Nguyen meekly took out a second packet.

'What is this?'

'Heroin.'

The baby-faced trafficker was in possession of just under 400 grams of the stuff—enough to hang him twenty-six times. Under Singapore law anyone caught with more than 15 grams of heroin faces a mandatory death penalty. Four hundred grams would have netted several million dollars on the streets of Sydney and Melbourne—at the time of Nguyen's arrest a heavily diluted gram would fetch A$300 to A$400. Drug addiction had long been a major social scourge in Australia—and an easy money-maker for some. Syndicate bosses, mostly Vietnamese, were becoming multimillionaires almost overnight. It was a business many wanted to get into. At the same time addicts and their families were suffering from the drug's destructive influence. Turf wars broke out regularly between the drug gangs, creating yet more havoc.

I watched Nguyen's case unfold in the High Court and was there the day the verdict was announced: death by hanging. His trial began in early 2004. The evidence was clear and damning. In statements read to the court, Nguyen claimed he was just a drug mule, involved in a one-off attempt to make some quick money. He told investigators he and twin brother Khoa had serious financial problems. He claimed Khoa was in deep with a Melbourne loan shark. Nguyen Van Tuong's intention was to use the $40,000 he would receive for the drug run to settle their debts. Despite his evidence, there was no proof I know of that Khoa knew of Van's activities or that he was to profit from his brother's activities.

As she busied herself in her Melbourne kitchen after returning from work, Kim Nguyen was soon to learn all about the purpose of her son's 'holiday' trip to Cambodia. The Australian Federal Police had received a phone call from Singapore. Officers raided the bewildered woman's home just before midnight. Her son had been arrested at Changi Airport for drug trafficking. It was serious, they told her. Her son was facing the death penalty. They also had a warrant to search his bedroom and the rest of the house.

I'd moved to Singapore from the United States about the time of Nguyen's arrest and kept track of the case and pending trial. One of Australia's biggest magazines, *Woman's Day*, commissioned me to write a special feature about the many Australian citizens held in prisons across Asia—Vietnam, Hong Kong, Laos, Cambodia, Thailand, Brunei and Indonesia—serving long sentences or awaiting execution. Schapelle Corby, a twenty-seven-year-old Australian woman, had just been arrested for taking 4.2 kilograms of marijuana into Bali and Nguyen's appeal was to be heard twelve days later. Both were wondering whether they would die—Nguyen on the gallows, Corby in front of a firing squad. There were scores of their fellow citizens rotting away in filthy prisons, some also fighting for their lives or begging for leniency, some forgotten and some wishing they had never been born. The threat of being strung up, shot or given impossibly long prison sentences in the most sordid conditions didn't seem to have been any kind of deterrent. These people were mostly fools, too naïve for their own good, putting their lives on the line at the most ridiculous odds.

Nguyen was an unknown quantity to me at that time. Would this be another controversial case that would reverberate across Australia and perhaps the world, stirring anti-death penalty campaigners into action again? Because of its death penalty laws, eyes are often focused on Singapore whenever news gets out that they are about to hang someone, especially if it's a Westerner. To get a better picture of some of these characters, I boned up on the trial reports and executions of Australians Kevin Barlow and Brian Chambers, who were hanged in Malaysia in 1986 for trafficking 141.9 grams of heroin. Next was British-born Michael McAuliffe, a barman from Sydney. He was executed in Malaysia in June 1993 after languishing for eight years on death row while going through a tortuous appeals process. McAuliffe was arrested at Penang International Airport with a large stash of heroin packed into condoms in his money belt. While looking into these old and new cases, I met up with an Australian Federal Police (AFP) narcotics agent based in Singapore.

'Why on earth do they take such risks?' I asked him.

'If you find out, let me know,' he replied dryly.

Nguyen's defence lawyers claimed at the trial he had given police helpful leads to track down the Melbourne syndicate and the Cambodia connection. He deserved a break. But in court a CNB agent said he had only wasted their time with false leads.

According to Nguyen, the plan was for him to transport a 'package' from Phnom Penh to Melbourne or Sydney via Singapore. He said he was given several thousand dollars to cover the air fares and accommodation. When he arrived in Phnom Penh he was met by members of a drug syndicate. He described a dramatic cat-and-mouse game, getting last minute instructions via mobile phones, moving from one meeting point to another to make sure he was not being tailed by narcotics agents until they were satisfied Nguyen was 'clean'. He was taken to a secret hideout, a backstreet garage, shown how to crush heroin crystals and divide them into two packets that would be taped onto his back. He then made a first-ever trip to his ancestral homeland, Vietnam, for some sightseeing in Ho Chi Minh City. He also sought the company of prostitutes but during his interrogation Nguyen claimed he did not have sex with them. Even though he knew then he would never see his girlfriend in Melbourne again, perhaps he was being gentlemanly by not revealing such an indiscretion.

Back in Phnom Penh several days later he met up with his contacts again. He was late for the appointment but his explanation was accepted. The heroin was ready to be crushed and packed. He went back to his hotel and prepared for the trip home. The journey would take him through Singapore. He boarded Silk Air flight MI622. The arrangement back in Australia was that a stranger would approach him, start a conversation and then suddenly say: 'I like basketball.' The deal would be done. Nguyen would get his money. Some of it would go to his brother. Their problems would be solved. That was his story. It seemed all too simple.

Halfway into the journey, however, Nguyen's nerves were getting the better of him. He fidgeted. He had difficulty breathing. One of the tapes binding the heroin packets had become loose and uncomfortable, slipping gradually down his back. He headed for the toilet to make some adjustments but the packet fell into the aisle as he got out of his seat. Inside the toilet he tidied himself, then returned and slipped the troublesome packet into the haversack in the compartment above his head. There was nothing more the judge needed to hear. Nguyen had been caught red-handed. The traditional black cap was placed on the judge's head. Nguyen was ordered to stand.

'The sentence of this court upon you is that you will be taken from this place to a lawful prison to be hanged by the neck until you are dead. And may the Lord have mercy on your soul.'

Nguyen was bundled down the steps to a holding cell below the courthouse to await a police vehicle to take him back to Changi Prison. A new cell was being prepared for him. He would now be on death row.

Seven months later, on 30 October 2004, his appeal began. As I arrived by taxi to report the proceedings, I could see wide-berth boats floating along the Singapore River full of tourists, relaxing happily in the warm sunshine. Inside the grim, packed court room three appeals judges in traditional robes were about to issue their decision in a terse, 90-second statement. I was sitting next to Nguyen's mother in the public gallery. Kim Nguyen, hands clasped throughout the hearing, was quietly praying, while staring down at her son, a lone, tiny figure in the dock, with two guards on each side armed with guns. Nguyen looked intently at the judges, trying to read their faces as they came and went and returned again to announce the verdict. He occasionally turned his head to make eye contact with his terrified and tearful mother. When the verdict was announced and the judges quickly filed out of the court room, Mrs Nguyen buried her face in her hands and sobbed as she took in what it meant. A young lady from the Australian High Commission tried to comfort her. Her son had just lost another battle for his life. His only hope was the President. But his appeal for clemency was denied. The appeal was based on various technical grounds: Nguyen was not given access to a lawyer to represent him while he was being interrogated. His lawyers also argued that the mandatory death penalty in Singapore was contrary to international law. That was dismissed because Singapore had not signed any international agreement on this issue. It was a foregone conclusion.

Even then, Nguyen's case received scant coverage in the Australian media. After all, to the majority white population he was just another Vietnamese immigrant bringing deadly drugs into his adopted country. However, one Australian internet blogger and controversial anti-prohibition campaigner, the late Gary Meyerhoff, could not contain his rage. 'In stark contrast to events in 1986 [when Barlow and Chambers were executed],' Meyerhoff wrote, 'Van Tuong Nguyen has been virtually ignored by the Australian Government and the media.' Meyerhoff went on:

> Nguyen Tuong Van is definitely not a household name. Why is the media ignoring him? Is it because they can't pronounce his name or is the real reason a little more insidious than that? Schapelle Corby doesn't exactly roll off the tongue and she has been turned into a media celebrity, not to mention the millionaire Aussie yachtsman Chris Packer, recently released from an Indonesian jail after serving three months for failing to declare firearms. With regards to media reporting, there is obviously some sort of double standard at play. Brian Chambers, Kevin Barlow, Chris Packer and Schapelle Corby all have one thing in common. They are all white Australians. Nguyen's crime is that he is an Australian of Vietnamese origin. Australia's predominantly white journalists (and our white Prime Minister) have written him off as just another Viet boy dealing smack.

Meyerhoff's barbs may have pricked a few sensitive spots and attitudes began to change a little when photos of Nguyen's distraught mother outside the old Supreme Court building went out on the wires after his appeal was dismissed. But the name Schapelle Corby was still hogging the headlines. Not surprising, either. With photographs of her on the covers, *Woman's Day* and *New Idea* were flying off the shelves, selling more copies than Angelina Jolie, Brad Pitt and Nicole Kidman put together. Nguyen Van Tuong didn't stand a chance of getting his voice heard or his photograph appearing anywhere. He was hardly on anyone's radar screen.

But all that changed when I obtained an interview with the man who was to hang him. Nguyen was about to become another household name and enter the consciousness of all Australians, for better or worse. He was the first Australian citizen ever to be sentenced to death in Singapore and the prospect of his execution was gradually awakening human rights activists again down under and around the world. Australia had long ago abolished the death penalty as cruel and inhumane. Back home, Nguyen would most likely have got a prison sentence of twenty-four years with a third off for good behaviour. At twenty-five, he would have had time to reshape his life, learn his lesson and become a responsible member of society. But in Singapore, such thinking is unfamiliar, despite Changi Prison's proud motto: 'Captains of Lives: Rehab, Renew, Restart.' Unbelievably, these words are printed at the bottom of each letter sent to families by the prison governor announcing the day their loved one will be put to death.

As expected, my interview with the hangman added fuel to the growing furore as the execution day loomed nearer. When it hit the front pages, Joseph Koh, then Singapore's High Commissioner in Canberra, was on the phone to his Foreign Minister in Singapore with accounts of the potentially damaging interview he had just read with horror and dismay. Australia's Foreign Affairs Minister at the time, Alexander Downer, made a statement saying he said he was 'outraged' over Singh's comments and said that the hangman 'should get a decent job'. Of course, it had put Downer firmly in the hot seat as many of his fellow citizens were horrified at what was about to happen and wanted him to do something more to help save Nguyen's life. Many Australians demanded he get tough with obstinate Singapore by threatening an economic boycott and diplomatic reprisals.

As anti-government feelings were increasing and with an election coming up the following year, Prime Minister John Howard would come under fire as a result of another interview I obtained—this time a joint interview with Mike McKenna, a reporter from the *Australian*, speaking to renowned criminal defence lawyer Subhas Anandan. During the interview Anandan revealed one of Singapore's best-kept legal secrets—that there is no separation between the executive and the judiciary. He said that if the Australian government had intervened in Nguyen's case the moment he was arrested, his life might have been saved. The charges could have been reduced at executive government level with a little tweaking of the facts, as had been done in several of the cases I investigated. I inferred that, although Howard may have been aware of the nuances of Singapore law, he was not interested in saving the Melbourne man's life at any cost. During the interview Anandan criticised Australia's eleventh hour tardiness in coming forward only after every legal process had been exhausted, including an appeal to the President for clemency. He described it as 'like visiting a patient in hospital when he is already dead'.

What was never revealed after Nguyen's arrest and during his trial was that he had set out on his ill-fated trip completely oblivious to the fact that he was walking into a carefully laid trap. His activities as a drug trafficker were already known to Australia's Federal Police drugs unit even before he left home. Nguyen was shadowed everywhere he went from the moment he agreed to take on the perilous assignment. Knowing his plans in advance, the police watched him leave his home in Melbourne early that December morning for the airport, where he bought a return ticket to Phnom Penh via Singapore. He was watched closely when he arrived at Changi Airport. Singapore's Central Narcotics Bureau agents knew he was coming, too. Then he was watched boarding a connecting flight to Cambodia. The Bureau immediately called their counterparts in Phnom Penh, where the surveillance was taken up by undercover agents instructed to gather every bit of information about his movements, where he went, what he did and everyone he met.

Although he did not have a criminal record Nguyen had already attracted the attention of Melbourne police. He frequented sleazy bars and nightclubs and had begun dealing in drugs with his twin brother. Khoa, himself a convicted drug trafficker, was also suspected of being involved in organised crime and was under almost constant police surveillance. In 1998, over what was believed to be a turf war, he attacked a teenager with a samurai sword, seriously wounding him. The case did not come to trial until 2002, by which time Van was in custody in Singapore facing the death penalty. Khoa was sentenced to three years in jail for the attack. His teenage victim ended up in a wheelchair and spent months in hospital undergoing a series of operations. Khoa, the court was told, had left home against his mother's wishes, abused drugs and alcohol, and gambled.

The AFP has a well-established special liaison system with their counterparts in Singapore, Cambodia, Vietnam, Indonesia, Brunei, Laos and the Philippines, with a declared aim to make Southeast Asia drug-free by 2015. Exchanging information about the cartels and their mules is a vital part of their operations. How Nguyen was caught red-handed was revealed to me by a newly retired CNB officer. I always had a nagging feeling that the real story had not been told and it took many phone calls and visits to bars where I learned some CNB officers hung out. Finally, I was introduced to my informant, who was prepared to talk on condition of anonymity. We met at Galbiati's Italian deli restaurant at the Rail Mall on Upper Bukit Timah Road in Singapore for lunch on a quiet afternoon. After assuring him that I was not wired nor had a hidden tape recorder, he told me that he was still with the Bureau when Nguyen was arrested and although he did not work on his particular case he knew all its inner workings. It was no chance happening or bad luck on his part. Nguyen was caught through a carefully planned, top secret operation. The AFP knew all about the drug run. Both Khoa and Van had been under surveillance, the AFP using undercover agents, paid informants and tapped phones for months. The object was to identify everyone involved and all their cross-border connections. No one was completely sure where Nguyen was going or who he would be dealing with once he left Australian shores. The syndicate's plan might be changed at any time. And Nguyen might change his plans and bring the drugs into Singapore instead of Australia.

The surveillance operation became more complicated when Nguyen suddenly decided to visit Vietnam. His mother had escaped with her husband in a perilous boat journey when America's war finally came to its ignominious end. Nguyen was born in a refugee camp in Thailand and the family moved to Australia when he and Khoa were tiny tots. This was his first trip abroad since then and the closest he had been to his ancestral land. He arrived in Phnom Penh just after midday on 3 December 2002 and immediately checked into the S$50 a night three-star Cara Hotel in the city centre. Then he headed for a pre-arranged venue, the Lucky Burger restaurant, at 3 pm the next day.

Nguyen told his Singaporean interrogators that he was taken to a garage where he was questioned by his new suppliers. They were suspicious of him, too. In true Hollywood movie style, he was ordered to smoke some heroin to make sure he was 'for real'. He claimed he refused and only obeyed them when they threatened him with an iron bar. He also claimed they had to show him how to crush rocks of heroin and safely strap the powder concealed in packets to his body. He was then told to meet them at the same fast food restaurant again six days later on 10 December. He now had time on his hands so decided to fly to Ho Chi Minh City for some sightseeing and to buy some Christmas presents for his family and friends. As soon as he checked into the airport, Vietnamese undercover agents were on his trail but with orders not to arrest him under any circumstances. No one could be sure of his motives in going to Vietnam or who he might meet there. 'He was watched everywhere he went,' said my informant. 'He didn't suspect a thing.' As it turned out Nguyen's trip to Vietnam was an innocent excursion, but it caused him to miss his appointment by one day. The syndicate leader was furious but finally accepted his excuse. Nguyen was then given the consignment of heroin and returned to his hotel, where he divided it into two packets, each weighing almost 2 kilograms.

He was so nervous on the flight to Singapore that one of the packets strapped to his back became loose. When it slipped off and fell into the aisle as he went to the toilet, he became even more nervous. He must have felt certain he was being watched—if not by an undercover agent, then by a member of the syndicate. He eyed the passengers on his way back to his seat. 'One of our men was actually sitting just a few rows behind him,' said my informant.

The day after Nguyen's arrest, the CNB issued the following statement:

On 12 December 2005 at about 19.45 hours, as part of stepped-up security checks at all checkpoints, CIAS Auxiliary Police at Changi International airport conducted a routine check on a 22-year-old male Vietnamese of Australian nationality at the boarding gate. Upon checking him, they found a packet of heroin weighing about 382 grams strapped to his back. He then informed officers that there was another packet of heroin in his hand-held haversack bag. Upon searching the haversack, a packet of heroin weighing about 380 grams was seized. The case was then referred to CNB for investigation. The male Australian ... will be charged in court for possession of a controlled drug for the purpose of trafficking. Under the *Misuse of Drugs Act*, a person who is found guilty of possession for the purpose of trafficking in more than 15 grams of heroin will face the death penalty ... In view of the current global situation ... drug traffickers can ... expect to face a heightened gauntlet of security checks and measures at our entry and exit points.

According to court papers, the money Nguyen claimed he was being pressured for totalled only A$25,000. Khoa's urgent debt was a mere A$12,000. By his own admission, Nguyen could earn A$25,000 a year in a regular job. It seemed relatively small money to risk one's life for. And it seemed an unlikely story. I was introduced to the former CNB officer just as I was completing research for this book. I wanted to dig deeper into Nguyen's inexplicably dangerous drug run. Was he really such a hapless, desperate mule or someone trying to get into the big time with Khoa? There was no real defence except some wrangling over legal technicalities: were his rights infringed when he was interrogated without a lawyer present; should the mandatory death penalty apply in his case; did his five separate statements amount to a confession? Was the CNB derelict in not informing the Australian High Commission earlier of his arrest? Is execution by hanging cruel and unusual punishment? The arguments were dismissed by the trial judge and later by the three court of appeals judges. Nguyen had been caught red-handed. He had admitted the crime. He would be hanged. Nguyen was moved to a cell on death row as soon as he returned from the Supreme Court on 20 October 2004.

Cameron Murphy, President of the New South Wales Council for Civil Liberties, revealed what he calls 'Howard's death penalty shame'. After the Howard Liberal government was defeated in the 2007 election and Kevin Rudd became Prime Minister, Murphy wrote this on the New South Wales Council for Civil Liberties (NSWCCL) official website:

After two years, the Australian government has finally released confidential documents about Australia's death penalty policy. The

Freedom of Information documents show that the Howard government deliberately set out to undermine Australia's opposition to the death penalty. Australia has an international obligation not to expose any one in any circumstances to the real risk of execution. What these confidential government documents show is that since 1998 Australia has been deliberately breaching those obligations.

Murphy went on to point out that: 'In the late 1990s, the Howard government decided that Australia could assist in foreign death penalty cases without a guarantee that no one would be executed. This violates Australia's international obligations and was a significant break with past practice.' Elsewhere Murphy pinpointed the way that:

the confidential internal documents show that the Howard government made a conscious decision to 'revise' Australia's universal and consistent opposition to capital punishment 'in light of the government's strong stance on terrorist offences'. Australia has a longstanding principled opposition to the death penalty. Australia respects the right to life of all individuals—no matter their crime. We should not be assisting in the court cases of people who could be executed. The confidential documents show that the government had flawed legal advice stating that Australia's human rights obligations do not extend beyond our borders or beyond individuals in the custody of Australian agents overseas. This advice is clearly wrong. It is inconsistent with Australia's obligation not to expose anyone in any circumstances to the real risk of execution ... We welcome the new openness of the Rudd government and thank it for finally releasing these documents.

When Howard was being urged in parliament to try to save Nguyen, he replied: 'I have told the Prime Minister of Singapore that I believe it will have an effect on the relationship on a people-to-people, population-to-population basis.' He did not say prime minister-to-prime minister, government-to-government or business-to-business relationship. Howard had rejected calls for trade and military exercise boycotts against Singapore, one of Australia's strongest allies and trading partners in Asia. He only said that the execution should serve as a warning to other young Australians: 'Don't imagine for a moment that you can risk carrying drugs anywhere in Asia without suffering the most severe consequences.'

6

FINAL DESTINATION

It was just another Friday morning. Singaporeans were waking up, getting ready for work and preparing for the crowded trains and highways to get to their offices, stores and factories. Few were aware that just as the sun rose the life of Nguyen Van Tuong had come to a brutal end. But where was the man who hanged him? Singh had seemingly vanished from his home in Woodlands. He had not been seen for several days. The rumour mill was grinding out the story that he had been sacked for breaking the *Official Secrets Act* in talking to me. Soon after I had exposed him as the much-feared executioner, his normally quiet neighbourhood was suddenly besieged by television crews, reporters and photographers anxious to get another interview, another photograph. They had camped out in the street below his tenth storey flat. He could not go out for fear of being followed and badgered for more of his secrets. He was afraid of being filmed every time he showed his face.

At 3 pm on 30 November, two days before the execution was scheduled to take place, plain clothes officers from Changi had picked up Singh and his wife and taken them to a furnished flat in a guarded compound adjoining the prison where guards and their families reside. Only a few hours earlier, highly distressed at having his world turned upside down, Singh told me he had complained to the prison governor that he was unable to move outside his home without being followed everywhere by Australian and international paparazzi. To avoid further embarrassing revelations and an 'unseemly' convoy of the world's media following him to the prison the morning he would hang Nguyen, the authorities decided that he and his wife should be moved.

Small groups of civil rights campaigners held candlelight vigils all night. They were careful not to number more than four—otherwise they could be arrested for 'unlawful assembly'. But there was little the authorities could do about them. The media had swelled the numbers until I counted at least 120 reporters, television crews with their producers, presenters and photographers. The area was lit up like a film set. Some of those in the milling crowd that lined the perimeter fence of the prison were undercover police taking notes and photographs just like everyone else. It was difficult to distinguish who was who unless you knew them. Some were reporters from the *Straits Times*, known for employing reporting staff straight from government intelligence and spy units. They were not looking for stories but the storytellers. Their reports only appear in files on people they believe they need to keep regular tabs on.

The ruse to get Darshan Singh inside the jail to carry out the execution worked beautifully. He was up early. It was 4 am. No one noticed the plain-looking car that took him along Tanah Merah Besar Road, almost under their noses, drove through the gates and disappeared into an underground car park beneath the prison cells where Nguyen was waiting. Death for the young Australian was only minutes away. Soon he would be on his way to the gallows. Singh peeped through an eye-hole to observe his demeanour. He was dressed, sitting on the edge of the concrete slab that served as his bed, hands clasped in prayer. He appeared calm thanks to the sedatives I was told he had been given with his last meal the previous evening. The day before I had called the public relations duty officer at the Ministry for Home Affairs for confirmation that the execution would go ahead as planned. There was no response, in keeping with their rule that they do not provide such information about who is likely to be hanged and when.

Even the families of those facing the gallows receive scant notice, and any information about the Friday hangings is typically released only after they have been carried out. Nguyen's mother, Kim, had received a letter from the prison governor a week before, abruptly informing her of the date he was to be hanged.

The callous way Singapore officialdom treats families angers Tim Parritt, spokesman for the human rights watchdog Amnesty International. 'They are in a state of complete anxiety and lack of knowledge until very, very late in the day.'

As the dawn sun was slowly rising, Nguyen's life was about to come to an end. He had already said his goodbyes to his heartbroken mother, Kim Nguyen, his twin brother, Khoa, and friends Bronwyn Lew and Kelly Ng in the visitors' area in Changi Prison the day before. Singh entered his cell at the prescribed time. The two already knew each other well. Singh had visited the 'baby on death row', as he'd been dubbed by his condemned 'neighbours', several times over the previous weeks, mainly to weigh and measure him, but also to put him at ease during the countdown to when the time came to put him to death. He treated Nguyen in the same gentle way he had always done with those he was about to hang.

As he had done hundreds of times, Singh pinioned Nguyen's arms behind his back with straps and handcuffs and led him out of the cell to the execution chambers a dozen or so steps away. Once he was standing firmly on the twin trap doors, following the usual rule, Nguyen's legs were strapped together. Nguyen went quietly to his death, long resigned to his fate. His execution took place at exactly 6.07 am. He was officially reported as dead at 7.17 am. In a blunt statement a Ministry of Home Affairs spokesman said: 'The execution was carried out this morning at Changi Prison.' Later that day, at around 3 pm, Darshan Singh and his wife arrived back home. The ordeal was finally over for them, too.

The moment Nguyen was hanged on that Friday morning, 2 December 2005 in Singapore, the bells at St Ignatius Catholic Church in Richmond, Melbourne, which his mother regularly attended, began to ring out twenty-five times—one for each year of his life. Many Australians wore yellow ribbons as a gesture of support and mourning and protesters in Canberra held placards proclaiming: OH SINGAPORE HOW COULD YOU. Meanwhile, Prime Minister Howard was at the centre of another storm of protest because he'd chosen to attend a cricket match in Canberra instead of calling it off out of respect for Nguyen and his family. Labor Senator George Campbell said Mr Howard's justification for attending Friday's game was feeble. 'I think it's an outrage that the match should go ahead and if he has any support for the abolition of hanging, he shouldn't go to the match,' Senator Campbell told reporters in Canberra. 'Instead, he should lead a protest in Parliament House against it. Of course call off the match. Of course, he's being insensitive.' Australian Democrats Senator Natasha Stott Despoja agreed, saying she felt sickened by the prospect that Howard would attend the game. 'This is about how Australians and the rest of the world, including the people of Singapore, will view our response to this horrendous act,' she said. Writer Mark Baker also attacked Howard and Downer in the Melbourne *Age*:

> In the island metropolis to our north, a place that admires itself through a polished veneer of modernity and sophistication, the city-state's brand of justice will be delivered with all the subtlety and compassion of the Middle Ages. At dawn on a Friday soon a young Australian will be taken from his death-row cell in the grey colonial pile of Singapore's Changi Prison, fitted with a hood and noose and dropped to oblivion through a gallows trap door. A few hours later his broken body will be handed back to his family. Yet few beyond his family, friends and dogged legal team are likely to mourn the passing of Nguyen Van Tuong, convicted heroin trafficker. As one of his Melbourne lawyers, Julian McMahon,

observed despairingly at the weekend, Nguyen is not the kind of pretty young Anglo-Saxon damsel whose distress ignites national indignation. But there are good reasons Australians should be alarmed and angered by the impending execution of the 25-year-old former Melbourne salesman—and why they should be demanding a much more vigorous response from the Federal Government to the final rejection of his plea for clemency than the limp resignation we are now witnessing from John Howard and Alexander Downer.

But Howard, who maintained all efforts to save Nguyen had been exhausted, said he had an obligation to host the Prime Minister's XI cricket match on the day Nguyen was hanged. 'I think the Australian people will understand that I didn't set the date of this man's execution,' said Howard. 'I wish there was no date set for his execution.' The Australian Labor Party, then in opposition, responded differently, calling for an economic boycott. Opposition Leader Kevin Rudd seemed to believe, like many others, including me, that international trade can, in the right circumstances, help decide who lives and who dies on the gallows in Singapore.

7

THE MIRACLE

The petite young Vietnamese woman with two small children looked every bit the doting mother. She bought them ice-cream and they sat happily in the transit lounge at Changi Airport waiting for a connecting flight to Perth. Now an Australian citizen, she was returning from a two-week trip to her homeland, ostensibly to let her ageing mother in Ho Chi Minh City see her grandkids for the first time. The Singapore Airlines flight that brought her from Ho Chi Minh City had landed at Changi Airport thirty minutes earlier.

While she sat in the lounge with son Kenny, almost four, and daughter Vanessa, almost two, her two suitcases were being transferred to another Singapore Airlines flight that would take them back to Australia. Airport security officers were walking along the rows of suitcases, trunks and backpacks with a team of dogs specially trained to detect anything dangerous—explosives, bombs and prohibited drugs, especially heroin, cocaine and opium. They were carrying out their routine searches to ensure that not a single piece of luggage is loaded onto any aircraft before it's thoroughly checked. There are never exceptions. Singapore is one of the biggest trading and tourism hubs in the world with the most efficient terrorist security and drug detection systems to be found anywhere. The flight would take the Vietnamese woman and her family on to Perth, arriving at precisely 12.26 am on 28 February 2006. They would then board a domestic flight that would take them back to Sydney. Home again, safe and sound, where she would be reunited with her other son, Billy, aged eight.

This is the incredible story of Thi Thanh Nga Ho, a thirty-seven-year-old divorced mother who, as if by a miracle, managed to escape detection and inevitable execution—twice! For the sniffer dogs prowling the suitcases, nostrils flaring, seemed suddenly to have lost their sense of smell. Their sensitive noses can normally pick up and distinguish different odours almost instantly, but on this occasion they inexplicably failed them. Packed inside her specially made suitcase was a stash of pure heroin worth A$3.6 million on the streets of Sydney and Melbourne. The dog handlers, all members of an elite security unit, also found nothing suspicious. Or so it appeared. 'They don't miss a thing,' said a retired CNB officer of my acquaintance. 'It would be a miracle for anyone with that kind of contraband to get through Changi Airport undetected.'

So Ho, even if she didn't know just how efficient the security system was, must have breathed a very big sigh of relief when they let her through without question. Using small children as cover or distraction is a common ploy of some drug traffickers, but security officers gave Ho, Kenny and Vanessa just a cursory once-over when they walked through the metal detector, the final check before take-off. She was on her way home, her problems solved. Or so she thought. During the flight to Perth she must have considered how lucky she was to have got through security in Ho Chi Minh International Airport and again at Changi without a hitch. Had she been arrested in Vietnam or Singapore, she would very likely have suffered the same fate as Nguyen Van Tuong, hanged less than three months earlier. Depending on how many others were already on death row, she would have become another number to be hanged by Chief Executioner Darshan Singh.

The prospect of another Australian citizen—and a woman with three young children at that—being hanged in Singapore would have been a disaster for diplomatic, economic and cultural relations between the two countries. Even though John Howard's government did little to save Nguyen and refused to get tough with the Lion City if the execution went ahead, this would have been quite a different kettle of fish. On 22 February 2006, just six days before Ho's arrest, Singapore attacked Australia's decision to reject a bid by Singapore Airlines to fly the lucrative Sydney–US route. Howard, still in power, tried to defuse the criticism, saying there were 'good reasons' for the decision, which virtually guaranteed Qantas dominance of the route. It appeared to many Singaporean officials that the decision to shut the door on Singapore Airlines had worsened relations between the two countries since Nguyen's execution. Singapore's Transport Minister, Yeo Cheow Tong, described the decision as 'extremely disappointing … especially after more than 10 years of protracted discussions'. Yeo was quoted in the *Sydney Morning Herald*: 'Singapore has also been more than generous in facilitating the growth of Australian carriers to and beyond Singapore. It is disheartening to see that they have taken this and the warmth in our bilateral relationship for granted.' For his part, Foreign Affairs Minister Downer said Australian officials would soon hold talks with Singapore about how to develop closer ties. 'There are things they want from Australia, there are things we want from them, and we'll sit down and we'll have a good talk about those things in an appropriate and a private setting. We don't link executions to aviation policy.' But this response did not assuage Singapore's suspicions.

Then came another shock news report—this time from the Australian Broadcasting Corporation (ABC) just before Nguyen was due to be hanged—saying that Singapore's refusal to grant him clemency may have led to a military exercise in central Queensland being cut short. Former Rockhampton Returned Services League (RSL) president Keith Joyce was quoted as saying he had been told the Singapore Armed Forces had cut the exercise at Shoalwater Bay by a week, and 'are now due to fly out by December 2', the day that Nguyen was due to hang. Mr Joyce said there was concern about a possible backlash towards Singapore troops and added that Singapore's refusal to stop the execution was damaging valuable military relations. 'We have obviously a very close link with Singapore and if the pleas of our Government, of our Prime Minister and of our Foreign Minister aren't having any effect on them, it makes me wonder why we are so closely involved with them at all.'

In the authorised biography *Kevin Rudd*, published by Penguin in June 2006, Robert Macklin quoted the Labor leader saying that if he were elected prime minister his most important foreign policy objectives would begin with a campaign to rid the world of the death penalty: 'It doesn't matter whether we are talking about the death penalty in the United States, the Islamic Republic of Iran, or in the Republic of Singapore, Australia should get behind the Europeans, through the UN, to make every effort to abolish this form of punishment, once and for all, throughout the world, and for all time.' It was another strong hint to Singapore that things would be different if Rudd became Prime Minister. Elections were drawing close in early 2007 and the Howard government, already in turmoil, was at its most vulnerable. Singapore was carefully watching what was happening down under. The Lion City saw Howard as their best friend and ally. But the fallout from the execution of Nguyen made everyone very nervous and Howard's growing unpopularity with the electorate did not bode well. Would Australia finally get tough with Singapore over this sensitive issue? What if Ho was tried and sentenced to death right in the middle of the election campaign? It would have been a bombshell. Leaders in both countries, it seemed, suddenly found it expedient to let Ho continue her journey home and be punished in Australia instead. It would avoid another but more devastating international row if Singapore was hellbent on hanging this young divorced mum with three little kids.

Can it be said that any Australian citizen found to be trafficking drugs via Changi Airport from now on will be let go to be dealt with in their own country's courts? As with other countries, which I will deal with in later chapters, is Singapore now open to ad hoc decisions regarding the death penalty for Australians for fear of a more serious rupture with the giant down under? At the time Ho was trying her luck, Howard was trying to regain his once dominant popularity. If Singapore had tried and sentenced her to death and he didn't do enough to save her—as many believe happened with Nguyen—this would have put an end to his already precarious political hopes. But whatever was going on, Ho was oblivious to it all. She was out of danger and on the way home. Just one more hurdle. That would be easy.

But Ho's relief at twice escaping inevitable execution quickly turned to despair when she arrived at Perth International Airport. Customs officers were waiting for her. They picked her out from the streams of passengers for a 'random' search. It was said that traces of an unidentified white powder were initially found just inside one of the suitcases. Traces of heroin that two teams of specially trained dogs strangely failed to sniff out? According to complete transcripts of her trial—initially denied to me by courts in Australia on the grounds that I was 'not an interested party' but now in my possession—it took forensic experts four hours to dismantle both pieces of her luggage. They found what they were looking for: four packets of heroin expertly wrapped with plastic and tinfoil. The terrified mother at first denied all knowledge of the heroin, but when she realised the game was up quickly confessed and cooperated fully with Federal Police narcotics officers. She even fingered an associate in Sydney as the organiser of the drug run. Court documents state that Ho had been given A$10,000 to cover airfares and accommodation for the family trip. If the run had been successful she would be paid A$40,000 per suitcase but later at her trial, when she pleaded guilty, she changed this to A$20,000, explaining the correct amount was lost in translation. She said she had had to leave her son Billy behind while she was gone. It was suggested in court that threats against the boy's security were used to ensure his mother went through with the arrangement.

Indeed, just as she was about to return with the heroin Ho got cold feet, telephoned her minder and asked if she could back out of the deal. She was told bluntly there was no backing out, as all mules are warned once they are in. More ominously, she was told Billy would not be safe if she pulled out. The A$10,000 advance for expenses would have to be repaid, and quickly. She was in too deep. When she first arrived in Vietnam, Ho said she met a male called 'Mai' who provided her with two brand new suitcases carefully packed with the heroin. She claimed she did not see this being done and had no idea exactly how much it was worth. On 27 February she flew back to Perth, stopping off in Singapore to catch a connecting flight.

Strange things happen often in the world of drug trafficking, the former CNB officer told me. Strange indeed if this woman was able to slip through two extremely efficient security nets, one in Ho Chi Minh City and one in Changi, only to be instantly picked out by customs officers in relatively sleepy Perth International Airport for a 'random' search. As soon as she was arrested, Chris Ellison, then Minister for Justice and Customs—as if on cue—issued an immediate statement praising Perth airport officials. It was the largest seizure of heroin at the border in Western Australia in twelve years, he said. A stash of 2.6 kilograms of heroin is no big deal in the wider world of drug smuggling, even in Sydney and Melbourne, but maybe it was in Perth and thus worthy of the minister's immediate attention. 'This seizure sends a clear message to those who attempt to import drugs that they will be caught.' The arrest and subsequent jailing of Ho for nine years in August 2006 received scant coverage in Australian newspapers. No one questioned that Singapore missed this one.

And did the media miss something bigger? Or was it simply glossed over by officialdom? My suspicion was aroused by attempts by two courts in Perth to prevent my seeing complete transcripts of the trial. Despite being a regular contributor to many Australian newspapers and magazines, I was told that as I was not part of the prosecution or defence nor was I related to the accused, I could not see them.

Fortunately—courtesy of an anonymous 'whistle-blower' perhaps concerned at this threat to freedom of the press—the transcripts turned up in the post at my home in Singapore.

So is it possible the authorities in both countries now have a secret, unwritten agreement that any drug trafficker passing through Changi on the way home will now be left to the Australian courts to deal with and thus avoid being hanged? And did an officer of the Central Narcotics Bureau—on orders of the Singapore government—call his counterpart in Canberra as soon as Ho boarded the homeward bound flight and say that she was on her way? Lawyer and human rights activist M. Ravi says that although it is impossible to prove that such an agreement has been reached between the two countries, the circumstantial evidence is overwhelming:

> The furore over the execution of Nguyen Van Tuong still resonates negatively with many Australians. No one in either country would want to risk going through a diplomatic and economic meltdown that would result if they hanged a young divorced mum with three kids. It would have been a very inconvenient execution. And if such ad hoc arrangements have to be made where someone's life is concerned what better reason is there to abolish the death penalty not only in Singapore but everywhere it is practised? The scales of justice would then be balanced for everyone—rich and poor alike. No one's life should be weighed against trade, business and diplomacy.

When Nguyen was hanged, anti-Singapore sentiment was at its highest in Australia. Threats of trade embargoes and deals concerning who lives and who dies on the gallows in Singapore should not shock or surprise anyone. And no one saying this should be prosecuted as I have been. While I was carrying out my research for this book, I discussed the case of Thi Thanh Nga Ho with a prominent Singapore criminal defence lawyer. At the time he disagreed with my theory that she'd been allowed to continue her journey to avoid another international squabble. But shortly after he read the first edition of this book he sent me an email saying: 'You were absolutely right—I made discreet inquiries and the authorities did know what was going on!'

8

80 MILLION GERMANS

German citizen Julia Suzanne Bohl, handcuffed and manacled, stood weeping in the dock, accused of possessing enough drugs to hang her several times over. Central Narcotics Bureau officers had been keeping her under surveillance for almost two months and had swooped on one of the two flats she leased during a wild party. They had reports that she was involved in trafficking drugs, and they were determined to catch her red-handed. Her arrest came during the early hours of 13 March 2002. She had 687 grams of cannabis in her possession—a traffickable quantity in Singapore.

Her wealthy but divorced parents, alarmed that she could end up on the gallows, had flown in from Germany to be at her side. With them came hordes of reporters, star TV news presenters and their camera crews. They piled into the court room and filled the grounds of the Subordinate Court to witness what could be the trial of the century back home in Germany, where the death penalty had long been abolished. The law in Singapore states that anyone found with 500 grams or more of cannabis must prove it was not in their possession for the purposes of trafficking, or be hanged. Julia Bohl looked like becoming another grim statistic for the hangman. Three Singaporeans nabbed with her in the raid—Mahdi Ibrahim Bamadhaj, twenty-three; Sunaiza Hamzah, twenty-three; and thirty-one-year-old Hamdan bin Mohammed—also faced similar charges.

It was a big, big story back in Bohl's native Germany. The very idea that one of their fellow citizens would be hanged for a drug offence was totally abhorrent to everyone in her country—and in the rest of Europe and many other parts of the world. In August 1994, Dutchman Johannes van Damme became the first European to hang in Singapore for drug offences, despite pleas for clemency from the Dutch government led by Queen Beatrix, the Pope and human rights organisations around the world. Van Damme was caught in 1991 at Changi Airport with 4.5 kilograms of heroin hidden in his suitcase. His execution left a lingering animosity between the two countries that persisted for years, damaging what had always been a harmonious relationship. So the seemingly inevitable execution of a Western woman looked like another huge international crisis in the making.

Within hours of being told of Julia Bohl's arrest and the awful consequences that might befall her, diplomats and lawyers in Singapore and Germany swung into action, working round the clock under the eye of Chancellor Gerhard Schroeder himself. The German Embassy hired one of Singapore's top criminal defence lawyers, Subhas Anandan, to take up Bohl's case and, indirectly, that of the Federal Republic as well. Much was at stake.

Everyone in Europe and top officials in the Singapore government remembered the outcry, followed by threats of economic reprisals against Singapore, when van Damme was hanged. Singapore recalled even more vividly the disastrous diplomatic and economic meltdown that followed the execution of Filipina maid, Flor Contemplacion. Germany was a major investor in Singapore and there might be catastrophic economic consequences if Julia Bohl were to be hanged. The Bundestag was in uproar and the tabloids were having a field day. When it was announced that Bohl faced execution, *Bild Zeitung* splashed a horrifying photo of her next to the gallows over almost the entire front page. The headline read: IF YOU HANG HER 80 MILLION GERMANS WILL HATE 4 MILLION SINGAPOREANS.

This story fuelled enormous public anger against Singapore and its people, so much so that anonymous death threats were sent to its then Ambassador in Berlin, Professor Walter Woon. *Bild Zeitung* has the highest circulation of any newspaper in Europe and wields significant political influence in Germany. If Schroeder did not move quickly and with a firm hand to save his precious citizen, it could cost him dearly at the next election. Singapore knew it was in danger, too. The small island nation, with its mandatory policy of hanging convicted drug dealers, would be brought into the international spotlight once again.

But what were the details of the case? Documents recording the judgment against Bamadhaj, one of the Singaporeans also charged, stated that Bohl and her boyfriend, a man known only as 'Ben', were using the Balmoral apartment to store drugs and drug-related supplies. For Bohl the good times came to a crashing, screaming end when dozens of armed CNB agents gatecrashed a party at her second flat at Goodwood Park. The mysterious Ben vanished into thin air, but Bohl, Bamadhaj and Hamdan were taken to her Balmoral Court flat by the CNB officers. It was later stated during Bamadhaj's appeal that this flat 'was often used for "drug parties" where ketamine and ecstasy were freely available'. Drugs and weighing scales were found on the premises. Under Singapore law, anyone found in possession of the keys to any premises where such drugs are found is presumed to have been in possession of those drugs. There is no presumption of innocence; it is up to the defendant to disprove their guilt.

Bohl's arrest made headlines in the media across Germany and all over Europe. It was widely reported that CNB officers had seized 687 grams of cannabis and other drugs from her apartment. In Singapore, 500 grams of cannabis is a traffickable quantity, meaning that the young German woman was facing the death penalty if found guilty. Bohl was initially charged with trafficking, and then additional offences including drug use, possessing ketamine and other drugs, and possession of utensils for their use. Possessing the ketamine alone carried a maximum sentence of ten years or a S$20,000 fine—or both.

But then, according to reports published by CNN and other media outlets, a chemist's analysis revealed that the block of vegetable matter found at the flat was not pure cannabis, but 'cannabis mixture', and when the block was analysed, the pure cannabis content was found to weigh only 281 grams—far less than the 500 grams that would attract the mandatory death penalty for this particular drug. Though Bohl still faced a jail term, it was a lucky escape.

An alternative version of Bohl's story was initially revealed to me by German journalist, Hommy Dara, who covered the case for *Stern* magazine and a TV station in Hamburg from the moment she was arrested. In the first edition of this book I did not print his name, as I did not wish to expose him, but in his indignation at my treatment by the Singapore government, Dara has since given me his express permission to make this fact public.

Dara introduced me to a recently retired CNB officer who told me, on the understanding that he would remain anonymous, that Bohl's activities had first come to the notice of the Central Narcotics Bureau following the so-called Orchard Towers Murders investigation. This was the case of Michael McCrea, a millionaire financial advisor who went on the run with his young Chinese-Singaporean girlfriend in 2002 when two bodies were found stuffed in a car in a car park at the high-rise shopping mall after a wild New Year's Eve party. Investigations into the murders ultimately led police and CNB agents to the activities of Bohl via her friendship with McCrea, who had by this time fled to England and then to Australia. As soon as they began investigating the crimes, the police and Central Narcotics Bureau realised they were on to something. Despite the furore created by the two murders just around the corner from her home, Bohl was totally oblivious to the fact that police had her under surveillance.

According to this anonymous source, it was not long after that Bohl was introduced to a good-looking young Malay-Singaporean man who said his name was Ben. Bohl took a shine to him, mesmerised by his good looks and charm. They soon became lovers and lived together in one of the two flats—but unknown to Bohl, Ben was an undercover police officer who had been ordered to befriend her in order to collect vital evidence that could be used to secure a conviction.

On the night of the party, the ever-present Ben hovered in the background as Singapore's beautiful people enjoyed themselves as Bohl's guests. At a pre-arranged time, her 'boyfriend' sent a signal on his mobile phone, and the CNB officers who had been waiting out of sight in unmarked vans and cars in nearby streets suddenly swooped.

'It's a dirty job but this is a dirty business,' the former CNB officer told me. 'We have to infiltrate the drug rings in this way. Otherwise they are closed to us. It's the only way we can get to know *them* and their activities and bring them to justice. The thing I always hated was that we had orders to encourage some mules to commit bigger crimes with more drugs than they planned to traffic. This meant sending them to the gallows—and many were. They would probably not have ended up that way if they had not been pushed or encouraged to do so.'

When Bohl eventually appeared in court for her trial, she was alone. Her tears had dried and her face was full of smiles. She had agreed to plead guilty to lesser charges that carried a maximum penalty of twenty years in jail and a $20,000 fine and, just as importantly, to give evidence for the prosecution and cooperate with the CNB by giving up names on her guest list. She received a sentence of only five years—a slap on the wrist in comparison to what happened to the likes of the Australian Nguyen and others.

Only one more of the four named in original court records ended up being prosecuted: Mahdi Ibrahim Bamadhaj. He was jailed for twenty years and given twenty-two lashes of the rattan cane. One of the chief prosecution witnesses was, as agreed, Julia Bohl. Her evidence cited him as the kingpin while she was under his influence all the time.

I tried to find out what happened to the other two Singaporean locals named in the original charges, but I had no luck. In Sunaiza Hamzah's case, perhaps she was allowed to fade into obscurity to avoid possible accusations that foreigners are treated more favourably than locals—especially if they are from a powerful country like Germany. For this young woman to end up on the gallows or be given a long, punishing jail sentence would have revealed more about Singapore justice than even the city-state could handle—despite its usual stance when things go wrong.

And what happened to Ben? According to a court document concerning Bamadhaj's appeal against conviction and sentence and after detailing the circumstances of the arrests: 'Ben is currently on the run. He was last seen by the CNB on the afternoon of 13 March 2002 at the car park at the York Hotel, after telling his friends present at the Goodwood Park serviced apartments that he felt he was being trailed by the CNB.'

Bohl was released in July 2005, having served only three years—just five months before Australian citizen Nguyen Van Tuong was hanged—and went to live in the Netherlands. When Nguyen was about to be hanged, shortly after Bohl returned to Europe, Singapore's Prime Minister Lee Hsien Loong said in a statement that he was sorry for Nguyen's mother that the execution had to go ahead. He pointed out that this was because the amount of drugs that Nguyen was caught trafficking to Australia via Changi Airport would have destroyed thousands of lives. What a contrast to the treatment Bohl received. Nguyen was merely using Changi as a hub, whereas Bohl's drug-related activities took place in Singapore's own backyard. It is not that Bohl should have hanged, but that Nguyen's life should have been spared, too.

'Julia has shown good behaviour in prison so she was granted a remission of one third of her five-year sentence,' prison spokeswoman Lim Soo Eng said on Bohl's release. Bohl, who had turned twenty-six while in jail, was immediately deported. She was picked up by her loving parents and consular officials outside the jail and immediately whisked back to the safety of Europe. Bohl was an ideal inmate, according to a prison officer. While serving her sentence, she was allowed to pursue a London School of Economics distance course in social science. Her privileged life in Singapore—she had wealthy parents and had completed her secondary studies at the local private German School—continued even while she was in prison.

The outcome of her trial astounded many human rights observers in Singapore but it was not until he published his memoirs in 2008 that her counsel, Subhas Anandan, revealed in more detail how it happened. He wrote:

> As soon as Bohl was caught, the German government and its ambassador in Singapore mounted a diplomatic offensive on her behalf, meeting several senior Singapore government ministers in the process. After negotiations with the Attorney-General's Chambers, Bohl still faced several charges but none was on trafficking in drugs and which were all subsequently dropped.

While these negotiations were going on *Bild Zeitung* and other tabloids were turning up the heat, signalling to Singapore just how appalled German citizens were at the prospect of Bohl being hanged. Anandan's memoir continued:

> I remember telling the Australian media just before his hanging that the only chance of saving Nguyen would have been before he went to trial, when the prosecutors were finalizing the charges and still had the prerogative to make changes. I told them: What is the point in coming in now? The President has already refused clemency and the presiding judge in capital drug cases has no discretion. Death is mandatory.

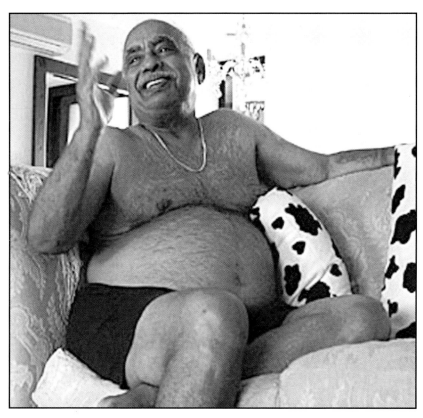

Darshan Singh: the Jolly Hangman. *Photo by Law Kian Yan, © Alan Shadrake*

Author Alan Shadrake poses for a photo outside the Supreme Court in Singapore for the original edition of this book. © *Alan Shadrake*

Alan Shadrake, accompanied by his lawyer M. Ravi, walks out of court in Singapore in November 2010 after being sentenced to 6 weeks in jail and a S$20,000 fine. © *Mohd Fyrol/AFP/Getty Images*

The Mourthi family will always grieve the loss of their only son and brother, Vignes, who was hanged for drug trafficking. © *Alan Shadrake*

Australian authorities refused to extradite British man Michael McCrea until the Singaporean government promised that he would not face the death penalty. Here he is shown arriving for his first appearance in court in Singapore. He was eventually convicted of culpable homicide.
© *AFP Photo/Ken Chow*

Top Singaporean criminal defence lawyer Subhas Anandan has represented many high-profile defendants, including Julia Bohl. © *Alan Shadrake*

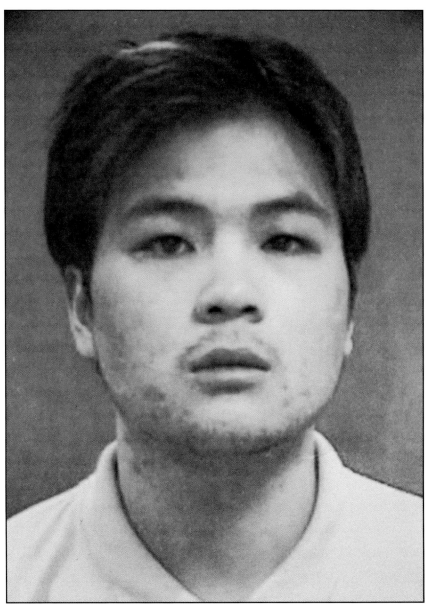

Nguyen Van Tuong's execution in 2005 caused a political backlash in Australia. © AFP Photo/Ho/Singapore Police Force

Protests against Nguyen's execution in Canberra, Australia.
©Tim Wimborne/Reuters/Picture Media

In Singapore, lawyer and civil rights activist M. Ravi demands an end to the death penalty just before Nguyen is hanged. © *Bob Low/AFP/Getty Images*

Protesters in Sydney, Australia, hold a silent vigil the morning of 2 December 2005 as Nguyen goes to the gallows. © *AAP Image/Mick Tsikas*

Shanmugam Murugesu's mother, Letchumi Ammah, breaks down at his funeral in 2005 after he is hanged for smuggling 1.03 kilograms of cannabis into Singapore. © AP Photo/Wong Maye-E

Shanmugam's mother, sister Mahes and brother Kuben grieve at his funeral.
© AP Photo/Wong Maye-E

German citizen Julia Bohl, in her Singapore German School Yearbook photo in
1997/1998. Four years later she would be arrested for possession of cannabis.
Her charges were eventually reduced and she escaped the death penalty.
© AP Photo/Singapore German School Yearbook

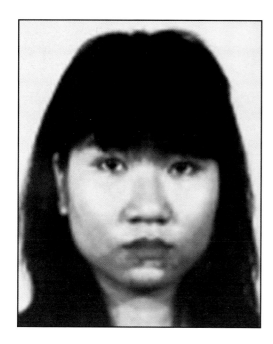

Angel Mou Pui-Peng, a Christian convicted of drug trafficking, was granted a two-week stay of execution so she could spend Christmas with her family. She was hanged in early 2005.

A candlelit vigil is held outside Changi Prison in 2007 to protest the execution of Nigerian footballer Amara Tochi. © *AFP Photo/Theresa Barraclough*

The execution of Filipino maid Flor Contemplacion in 1995 caused a breakdown in business and diplomatic relations between the Philippines and Singapore lasting almost three years. © *STR/AFP/Getty Images*

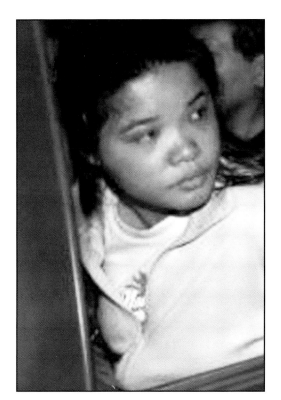

In 2005, Filipina maid Guen Aguilar (left) killed her best friend, Jane La Puebla (right), for reasons that remain a mystery. Aguilar escaped the death penalty.

Guiga Lyes Ben Laroussi, alleged supplier to the High Society Drug Ring, arrives at court for a pre-trial conference in December 2004. He would flee Singapore shortly afterwards. © *Roslan Rahman/AFP/Getty Images*

While the Australians were slow off the blocks in their diplomatic efforts on Nguyen, the German ambassador impressed me with his handling of the Bohl case. Volker Schlegel stood by Bohl all the way. He was a fantastic man, who gave me all the support and encouragement I needed. He would come to my office and we would spend hours discussing Bohl's case. I have acted for other nationalities and observed that the dedication shown by their ambassadors is not the same. Some can't be bothered if their nationals get into trouble in Singapore. Others only show an interest when the accused person is someone famous or important or well-connected. These ambassadors could have learnt a thing or two from Schlegel.

Although Nguyen and Bohl served roughly the same time behind bars, the young German woman was allowed to start her life all over again, and the Vietnamese-Australian man was hanged. Did race play a part in the outcome? Or didn't John Howard care enough to fight for Nguyen? How can the differences between these two cases be accounted for?

In an article explaining why Nguyen should be hanged, Asad Latif, a former senior reporter with the *Straits Times*, and a visiting research fellow at the Institute of Southeast Asian Studies in Singapore, wrote: 'Laws against drug trafficking must be implemented uniformly. No one has the right to expect, let alone demand, that Singapore bend its laws to suit the laws of another country.' Yet, as one Singapore lawyer told me: 'If the economy comes under threat from reprisals it will err on the right to life—and the right to trade—and buckle under from this kind of pressure.'

On the basis of claims I have made in this chapter, Judge Quentin Loh found me guilty in November 2010 of 'scandalising the judiciary'. Soon after news of my sentence was flashed around the world, I received an urgent phone call from Berlin. It was Hommy Dara, the German journalist who had covered the Bohl case in Singapore. Horrified at my conviction, he now gave me permission to reveal his name as one of my chief informants and offered to dig into his files for more evidence that justified my claim that Bohl received special treatment.

Dara told me that the German Ambassador had taken a hands-on approach to Bohl's case: 'He asked us not to attack the Singaporean government while high-profile negotiations were held behind closed doors.' Officials of the Ministry of Foreign Affairs asked all media chief editors to refrain from attacking Singapore and they agreed to do so. Dara added: 'When we asked if money was about to change hands, we were told: "No, not money in that sense but trade—investment benefits are legitimate tools in bilateral talks."'

Dara also told me that the German government had promised that certain German banks would invest heavily in Singapore—on condition that a 'diplomatic solution' was found to save Bohl. Unfortunately, I was never able to discover if these investments actually materialised and so cannot confirm that this theory has any basis in fact. Such sensitive financial information is impossible to find without breaking the law in Singapore.

But the deliberate suppression of the details of the case didn't stop there, according to Dara: 'There was a lot of clamour from the German media for Bohl's memoirs but she always refused. Part of the deal was her permanent silence. In fact, she refused all interview requests.' Dara told me that he had a brief from *Stern* magazine to offer Bohl up to 100,000 euros for an interview, but even this generous sum was turned down. Up to this very day, Bohl has not spoken a single word about what happened.

9

THE ODD COUPLE

One of the most bizarre stories I unearthed for this book concerned British financial adviser Michael McCrea, a reputed millionaire, and the aforementioned Julia Bohl. They were both involved in Singapore's elitist high society and, had their executions been ordered, Darshan Singh might well have hanged this 'odd couple' side by side. As it turned out, unlike hundreds of other criminals caught in Singapore sting operations and facing the mandatory death penalty, these lucky souls were spared the noose.

Bohl, aged twenty-three, and McCrea, forty-four, had long been close neighbours in a high-end part of Singapore—he in Pinewood Gardens, Balmoral Park, and Bohl just around the corner on Balmoral Road—where many foreign diplomats also reside. They first got to know each other through their mutual interest in the high life, frequenting various bars along the Singapore River.

Bohl grew up never having to work for her basic needs. When her parents had divorced and returned home to Germany to start separate lives, the young woman had elected to remain behind. Her allowance from her father alone was more than many medium-level executives earned in Singapore.

McCrea had a similar lifestyle. He was making pots of money persuading wealthy expats and Singapore's homegrown upwardly mobile executives to part with huge sums of cash that he would invest on their behalf. He advertised his services in glossy magazines and wrote an occasional column, 'Doing the Obvious Differently', for the *Expat* magazine in Singapore. (It was during this time that he became a close friend of the magazine's then editor, Nigel Simmonds, whose own arrest on a drug-related charge is discussed in chapter 15.)

Although married to an Australian who lived at their Melbourne home, McCrea enjoyed the company of young, glamorous women—including twenty-two-year-old Audrey Ong, who was to play a tragic role in his life soon after they met in 2001. They were introduced by McCrea's book-keeper, a young English woman named Gemma Ramsbottom, who had a second job at Pinkk, an exclusive bar in Club Street where Ong was a waitress. Not long after, Ong moved in with McCrea at his luxurious Pinewood Gardens residence.

McCrea was then making so much money that he was able to pay his live-in chauffeur S$6000 a month. Kho Nai Guan, aged forty-six, also doubled as his delivery and pick-up man, driving a Silver Daewoo Chairman 400 that McCrea had bought for him. McCrea would later tell his Melbourne lawyer, Terry Grundy, that Guan was 'like a brother' to him. Guan's salary was huge by local standards and in 2001 McCrea gave him a Christmas bonus of S$25,000. Just a few weeks later, McCrea would kill Guan and his Chinese girlfriend, twenty-nine-year-old Lan Ya Ming (also known as Suzie), in an outburst of rage. Michael McCrea's high life was about to come crashing down—but why?

According to Audrey Ong, McCrea had flown to Melbourne to spend Christmas 2001 with his wife and son. He never arrived because he was barred entry at the airport. Ong later alleged in her mitigation plea that he had been travelling under a false passport. She claimed that Australian immigration had received a warning from someone in Singapore and that McCrea suspected Guan, who knew all his secrets, might have reported him to the authorities. Back in Singapore, McCrea apparently tried to push these thoughts out of his mind and on New Year's Eve he was intent on enjoying himself with his friends. The next day he and Ong sat down with Guan and his girlfriend Lan to discuss their plans. McCrea said they should put their 'differences' behind them and make 2002 an even better year than 2001 had been. Then Guan and Lan decided to go to bed. Ong says that as Guan walked past he whispered to her in Hokkien: 'Don't talk too much, slut!' McCrea demanded to know what Guan had said, Ong translated for him, and a violent fight erupted between the two men.

The Briton was a fitness enthusiast, proud of his muscular physique. He had installed a full-size punching bag in the corner of his bedroom and he worked out every morning before breakfast. Guan was easily overcome and McCrea finished him off with blows from a metal rod. During the fight Lan went to Guan's aid, first trying to restrain McCrea and then coming at him with a knife and stabbing him in the hand as he tried to ward her off. McCrea knocked Lan unconscious with a single punch, kicking her as she lay helpless on the floor until she was unconscious. After attending to McCrea's wound, Ong and McCrea inspected Guan's body and realised he was dead. They then set about cleaning up the apartment while deciding what to do next.

Court records from her trial set out Ong's evidence of what followed: she said that McCrea became determined to find the large amount of cash he had recently paid to Guan as a bonus. Despite a long and thorough search, he did not find the money. The next day he interrogated Lan as she lay semiconscious on her bed. Whether he was successful in getting her to talk or not has never been established, not even during the trials that followed. The judge noted that investigations had revealed that McCrea had then placed plastic bags over Lan's head and secured the plastic bags with ties. As this was being done, Lan suddenly moved 'and appeared to be getting into a convulsion'. McCrea then suppressed her until she stopped moving.

Ong testified that she and McCrea called Gemma Ramsbottom and asked her to bring them cleaning supplies. They recruited another helper, Singapore nightclub barman Cheo Yi Tang, to help clean up the flat and and paint over bloodstains on the walls. Ramsbottom and Tang's involvement was later set out by each of them in sworn affadavits.

Ramsbottom told police that she, McCrea and Ong then drove around nature reserves, rainforests and the coastline, with Ong sitting in the back navigating, until it was getting light and they gave up on finding a suitable place to dipsose of the bodies. It was decided to leave them in the silver Daewoo saloon in a car park in Orchard Towers, a high-rise shopping plaza in a red light district best known for its sleazy nightclubs. McCrea and Ong then fled Singapore for Britain, where McCrea had a former wife, parents and siblings.

The bodies were found by a security guard and quickly identified. Warrants were issued for the arrest of McCrea and Ong, and their friends and associates were rounded up for questioning by homicide police. Officers of the Central Narcotics Bureau joined the investigation when blood tests revealed heavy drug and alcohol use by the victims shortly before they died. Homes and bars were raided, and it did not take police long to connect the dots. They soon realised they had uncovered an undreamt-of mine of information relating to an underworld drug scene—and in a bizarre twist, this information would eventually lead to the arrest of Julia Bohl, McCrea's Balmoral Park neighbour.

By now, though, the fugitive couple was out of reach. In London, McCrea had managed to obtain a false passport for Ong in the name Clare Reid, and they flew to Australia to stay with family, but Ong was denied entry, not because Australian customs officers were suspicious of an Asian woman with a typical Scottish name holding a British passport, but because she did not have a return ticket with her. It was with McCrea, who had already got through on his false passport. Ong then flew back to Kuala Lumpur, where she and McCrea had previously spent time, to decide what to do next.

She decided to go to Bali. Finally, after long telephone conversations with McCrea, she decided to attempt to join him in Sydney, this time using her Singapore passport. This time she was allowed in without a problem—she had that all-important return ticket.

They were caught out when, after a violent shouting match, police arrived unexpectedly at their door. While dealing with what they thought was a simple domestic dispute, the police discovered that McCrea had arrived in Australia using a fake passport. The game was up. McCrea refused to return to Singapore voluntarily and, because Australia cannot by law extradite anyone to any country where the death penalty might be imposed, a long legal battle ensued.

McCrea was eventually sent back to Singapore on condition that he would not face the death penalty. His two charges would eventually be reduced to culpable homicide, which carried a maximum penalty of ten years' jail each. In June 2006—seven months after Nguyen was hanged for trafficking heroin—McCrea was sentenced to a total of twenty-four years on the two charges plus four more for destroying evidence of the crimes. In effect, the death penalty for him had been abolished even before his trial began and Singapore did not like it at all. Lawyer Terry Grundy, who helped McCrea to fight his extradition, told me of the fury expressed by one of the Singapore lawyers he spoke to after the court decision: 'By the time we've finished with him, McCrea will wish he had been hanged!'

Despite being near neighbours and playing major roles in Singapore's party scene, Audrey Ong and Julia Bohl never met—until they ended up on the same cell block. Ong was released in July 2010 after eight years and very kindly agreed to meet me and help fill in some of the mystifying and confusing gaps in this saga. She told me: 'Everyone seemed to know everyone in our various party circles but I had never met Julia. But it nearly happened. One day a mutual friend came to the Pinewood Gardens flat to try to drag me to one of her poolside parties at the Balmoral apartment. I didn't go because I'd just got back from Melbourne in time for Christmas 2001. It was only about two weeks before that fatal New Year's Eve party that changed my life forever. It would have been my first meeting with Julia—before we finally ended up in Changi Prison together.'

By the time Ong and McCrea fled to England and Australia— stopping over for a three-week jaunt in Phuket—police had already discovered the Bohl connection through their mutual party-going friends in and around Balmoral Park. And by the time Ong returned from Australia voluntarily to face her charges, Bohl was also in custody.

'It seemed so strange,' said Ong, 'that because we had come so close during those wild party days that we finally ended up like that. When she heard I was on the same cell block but still had not seen each other she called out to me: "Audrey—I'm Julia Bohl." From then on we became good friends and would chat together whenever we had the chance. She reminded me of the invitation to her poolside party which I'd refused. But now we have been in touch again—by email. She has got on with her life and I want to do the same. No more drugs for me. I'm clean. She feels the same way. I just want to get back on track and settle down.'

Then Ong began talking about McCrea, revealing that she has twice talked to him since she was freed, each time via video-link to the prison. 'The first time I couldn't stop crying. It was very emotional for both of us. I no longer love him in the way I did, but I care for him and will always support him. He will likely spend another twelve years behind bars. I cannot wait that long. I want to marry eventually and have kids before I am too old.'

But if the tragedy of the Orchard Towers Murders had not taken place, perhaps Julia Bohl would never have been caught either. These two cases were followed by a third—for McCrea's arrest was the start of the amazing chain of events that resulted in one of Singapore's most embarrassing drug scandals being exposed.

10

SEND IN THE MARINES!

On 23 September 1994, a Dutch engineer became the first Westerner to be hanged under Singapore's draconian drug laws. Johannes van Damme went to the gallows despite appeals from Queen Beatrix, the Dutch Minister for Foreign Affairs Hans van Mierlo and the Pope. Van Damme, a handsome, burly man of fifty-six, claimed to be a secret agent in the employ of his country. Whether or not this was true, van Mierlo made a strenuous effort to save his life. The anti-Singapore sentiment that reached ferocious levels across the Netherlands shocked everyone. As preposterous as it seems, according to a national poll half the population demanded the government send warships to Singapore and rescue van Damme using military force. But Singapore ignored this wild expression of anger and all the pleas that came from the Netherlands, the rest of Europe and around the world. In a damning response, the Minister said his government and people were 'greatly disappointed and appalled to learn of the execution'.

Van Damme's execution coincided with the opening of ministerial talks between the Association of Southeast Asian Nations (ASEAN) and the European Union (EU) taking place in Karlsruhe, Germany. Van Mierlo was among the twelve EU ministers who attended the dialogue with their Asian counterparts. The execution had taken place only hours before the meeting opened. German Foreign

Minister Klaus Kinkel said in his opening address the EU regretted the execution, but the subject was not discussed during the ministerial meeting. The Singapore Foreign Minister, Shunmugam Jayakumar, said it would have been 'hypocritical' if they had changed the date deliberately so that it would not coincide with the meeting. To many human rights activists it suggested that the van Damme execution was another example of Singapore's resistance to Western pressure, when it suited them. Jayakumar explained that the execution was a matter of the law taking its course. He said that granting clemency on the grounds that capital punishment was anathema to the country of origin of an offender would undermine Singapore's integrity and reputation for impartial enforcement of the law. It would also be a serious breach in the Republic's battle against drug traffickers, who were 'worse than murderers'. 'A murderer normally kills one person, but a drug trafficker erodes the fabric of society,' he said. Referring to drug abusers in Singapore, he said: 'People are our only resource. And there are 8000 in drug rehabilitation wasting away, completely useless to our society until they are rehabilitated.' He went on to claim that 'the number of drug traffickers would have tripled or quadrupled if Singapore did not have the death penalty. It works for Singapore. We want to keep it.'

Van Damme was arrested at Changi Airport in September 1991 after 4.3 kilograms of heroin were found hidden in his suitcase. He had arrived from Thailand, a major shipment point for narcotics, the court was told, and was in transit awaiting a flight to Athens. A resident of Nigeria since 1976, he said that he had been set up by a Nigerian criminal operation he had exposed to the Dutch intelligence agency. According to newspaper reports at the time, his assertion of innocence had some credibility, particularly after the Dutch Foreign Ministry confirmed that he had been working with their intelligence agency up to the time of his arrest. The exact nature of those activities was not disclosed, however, and Dutch officials said they did not directly involve the drug charges in Singapore. This reticence should not surprise anyone: intelligence operations are usually steeped in secrecy. Van Damme, married to a Nigerian, said he had been carrying the bag for a Nigerian engineer and did not know what was packed inside the false bottom. According to an archived press report I found, van Damme's family in the Netherlands said they were 'completely in the dark as to what actually happened and can only conclude that other people deliberately or unintentionally involved him in the smuggling operation'. He was by nature law-abiding, they maintained. The family also released a copy of the usual bluntly worded telegram that they received from Singapore: 'Death sentence passed on Johannes van Damme will be carried into effect on 23.9.94. Visit him on 20.9.94. Claim body on 23.9.94.' It was signed by the superintendent of Changi Prison. But while foreign migrants and guest workers regularly ended up on the gallows for similar offences, van Damme's execution marked a significant ramping-up of enforcement at that time.

According to an Agence France-Presse report from The Hague, the then Dutch Prime Minister, Wim Kok, said the execution cast a 'grey veil' over his country's relations with Singapore. He revealed that the government had summoned the Singapore Counsellor, Kheng Hua Iseli, to emphasise the 'profound distress' they all felt. Kok said it was impressed upon Iseli that on both emotional and ethical grounds the Netherlands could not accept the decision to go ahead with van Damme's hanging. He said it demonstrated the cultural gap between the two countries and that he had urged Iseli to consider ways of bridging this gap by putting an end to 'these particularly inhumane judicial procedures'. The Prime Minister said his government had discussed whether there should be diplomatic and economic retaliation for the execution. But the idea was abandoned because such relations would have been restored after a few weeks or months anyway, with the risk of creating the impression that his country was wiping the slate clean.

Under the circumstances, this could have caused further

difficulties. By the strangest of coincidences, barely five months earlier another Dutch citizen, Maria Krol-Hmelak, aged fifty-seven, had been arrested in her hotel room in Singapore in possession of 1.6 kilograms of heroin. As far as I know, there is nothing to indicate that Krol-Hmelak and van Damme, both long time residents of Nigeria, knew each other. She was married but estranged from her Dutch husband, who had left her to live in Brazil. A few days earlier, in another Singapore hotel, a thirty-six-year-old Nigerian, Peter Johnson, was found with 0.33 kilograms of heroin. Both Krol-Hmelak and Johnson were working for a Nigerian trading company in Lagos called Kenrods Ltd. While Krol-Hmelak and Johnson were languishing in Changi Prison awaiting trial, van Damme's case was dealt with much faster and he was on death row sentenced to hang before their trials even began.

The Austrian-born Dutch citizen, Krol-Hmelak, had studied law, then economics, and finally became a chartered accountant. She was married to Frederik Krol and had a son by him named Christopher. Frederik Krol was a mechanical engineer and the family went to live in Nigeria to work for Kenrods in the 1980s. He travelled widely, often to Brazil to make contacts with Volkswagen and other car companies. While there in 1989 he found another job, resigned from Kenrods and left his wife and son. In April 1990 Maria Krol-Hmelak was persuaded to join Kenrods and was assigned to establish a branch dealing in coloured gemstones. At that time the gemstone business in Nigeria was booming. Many new minefields were being developed and new varieties of stones found. Nigeria had large deposits of sapphire, aquamarine, tourmaline, amethyst, emerald, garnet and crystal quartz. She obtained all the necessary permits and licences and began establishing a market in Germany. She soon found she could obtain better prices in Thailand and in October 1990 went to Singapore and Bangkok to obtain orders. However, Krol-Hmelak returned to Nigeria at the end of November to discover that the Middle East Gulf crisis was in progress and prices were falling drastically.

When the war began the bottom fell out of the market. One gram of good-quality sapphire that once sold for US$140 plummeted to US$20. At this time Krol-Hmelak was in Bangkok and was told to wait there until things improved, but when the war ended the market did not recover. It was not long after this that Krol-Hmelak suddenly found herself in trouble.

I have tried to find transcripts of her trial, but to no avail. I am not sure if these records even exist—so, in the following account, I rely on notes taken by P. Suppiah, her defence lawyer, who was kind enough to talk to me and share with me his memories of this case. It should be understood that the version of events that follows is that related in court by Krol-Hmelak, as recorded by P. Suppiah, rather than an impartial third-party record. But while I cannnot rely absolutely on these notes or vouch for their accuracy as I would a court transcript, I think it is worth hearing this woman's version of the events that befell her.

Krol-Hmelak said that her boss in Lagos told her to go to Singapore and await further instructions. Krol-Hmelak was hoping to be recalled to Lagos, where her son Christopher, then aged twelve, was being cared for by friends. But instead she was informed that Johnson, a new company director, was coming to Singapore for the first time. According to Krol-Hmelak, she was asked to stay on, check him into the Park View Holiday Inn, and show him around.

During one of her subsequent trips to Bangkok Krol-Hmelak says she received a call requesting that she collect several Caterpillar tractor engine parts and bring them back to Singapore. These turned out to be heavy pistons smothered in thick grease. In a statement she wrote in her cell for her defence lawyer, Krol-Hmelak said she had been taken to a second-hand spare parts shop in Bangkok in a tuk-tuk taxi. She waited in the cab while her contact there went inside.

'He returned shortly afterwards with a grey travelling bag,' she wrote. 'When I tried to lift it I found it very heavy. I looked inside and saw those greasy spare parts. He told me they were piston rings. At first I refused because they were too heavy.' However, since she was very eager to return home, Krol-Hmelak agreed. 'He said I would have to deliver them to a cargo company in Singapore for shipment to Nigeria. He said he would give me the name of the company later and I returned to my hotel. Then I remembered that I forgot to ask him for the invoice for the spare parts. I tried to reach him in his hotel, but could not.'

Krol-Hmelak returned to Singapore with the engine parts and briefed Johnson about her itinerary. He knew nothing of the pistons—or piston rings as she described them in her statement—and promised to call the office in Lagos because he wanted to know what was going on. 'The following evening he came to my room and asked for one of the engine parts because he wanted to find out more about it. I gave him one and reminded him to give me money for the hotel bill and other outstanding expenses.' Krol-Hmelak said she wanted to wind things up and finally return home to Nigeria but did not hear any more from Johnson. She called his room several times the following evening. There was no reply. A final call was answered by another person who passed the phone to him. Her statement continues:

> He told me he had been arrested because there was heroin in these machines. He said the police were with him. I was worried because I was left without funds and asked him to leave some money for me. Mr Johnson did not reply. He dropped the phone. Later I started wondering which machines he had with him that could have heroin inside, but I never connected the spare parts with it, simply because a spare part is just that: a part.

Krol-Hmelak said she then called the company in Lagos and informed them what had happened. 'I was very worried and upset because I was left in a bad condition, in a strange country without money to pay my hotel and my expenses. The company told me to hold on. They would send someone with money.' She waited six days and, the evening before her arrest, was sitting having coffee in a patisserie in Centrepoint shopping centre when it 'suddenly occurred' to her that Johnson was referring to the pistons she had in her hotel room. 'I then became very much afraid because I remembered the warning on the visa entry card for Singapore, that anyone carrying drugs can be sentenced to death. So I decided that though I was not sure that I was correct with my suspicions, the best thing for me was to throw them away.' She quickly obtained several black plastic bags from a nearby store and carefully wrapped the pistons separately, then together, and put them in a large travelling bag which she put in another plastic bag. 'By then I was feeling ill with stomach pains after I completed this task and decided to take them away the next morning even though an inner voice was prompting me to take the things away at once.'

The knock on her hotel room door came early the next morning. Officers of the Central Narcotics Bureau wanted to talk to her. 'I delayed opening the door,' she wrote for her defence lawyer. 'I was very scared and decided to try to hide the spare parts. I did not know where to hide them at first, but decided to put them in the sofa which converted into a spare bed.' It did not take the police long to find the hiding place. Krol-Hmelak was ordered to provide two urine samples. A week later, accused of being a drug addict, she claimed her interrogators were trying to frame her. 'I had never taken any kind of drugs,' she declared. 'You are framing me with that urine.' Despite her protests she was charged with one count under the *Misuse of Drugs Act*.

After van Damme was convicted, much to Krol-Hmelak's horror and the amazement of many, a Dutch newspaper, *AD*, published a report quoting a spokesperson for the Dutch intelligence bureau— Centrale Recherche Informatiediens (CRI)—accusing her of working with a Nigerian drug ring. 'The Dutchman J. van Damme, who has been sentenced to death in Singapore for smuggling heroin, is possibly part of a Nigerian drug ring,' said the spokesperson. 'The 59-year-old

Maria Krol, who has yet to be tried, would also have been drafted as a courier by a Nigerian drug ring.' The report also quoted Krol-Hmelak's estranged husband, who said that he intended suing the CRI for publicly portraying her in this way and at such a crucial time in the fight for her life. He was alleged in the report to have given to the American Drug Enforcement Agency (DEA) the names of Nigerians who were involved in smuggling drugs in 1989. Among those names were people who worked for Kenrods Ltd of Lagos—his employer until he resigned.

It was becoming very murky indeed. And it did not look good at all for Krol-Hmelak, a Kenrods employee at the time of her arrest. Her 'I didn't know' defence is used in 90 per cent of all drug possession cases, according to published records, and usually carries no weight at all, especially in Singapore. But she was being condemned in her own country even before her trial began.

When the inevitable verdict was announced in van Damme's case, the Dutch media began speculating on her fate as well. 'Death Sentence Threatens Dutch Woman,' *De Telegraaf*'s front page blazed. The trials of Krol-Hmelak and Johnson, despite objections from her lawyers, were held jointly. The first session before Judge Lai Kew Chai began on 23 September 1993. The sessions dragged on for six weeks with some lasting only a few hours, the two accused being shunted back and forth from their cells. The pair maintained all along they had no idea large amounts of heroin had been packed inside the spare parts.

There was one humorous, if somewhat bizarre, moment during the grim and tedious sixty-six-day trial. It had the court rocking with laughter. It happened when a police officer was giving evidence about Johnson's attitude when he was being questioned. Suddenly Johnson unzipped his pants, took out his penis and, in front of his interrogators, swore on it that he was telling the truth. It was as though he was taking a solemn oath on a holy book and claiming it was proof of his innocence—he would be prepared to have his penis cut off if he had lied. Johnson said it was an old Nigerian custom still used in his home country. Even the judge smiled, but some in the court room may well have wondered if Johnson was being brave or just plain stupid.

Following final submissions at the twenty-eighth session, which began on 29 October 1993, Judge Lai suddenly pronounced them both not guilty. Krol-Hmelak could hardly believe her ears. She was free. Completely stunned, she burst into tears, sobbing 'What's happening? What's happening?' By now she had been in jail for two and a half years, expecting she would end up on the gallows. Instead she heard cries from embassy officials: 'You are free! You are free!' It was an extraordinary end to the case. Her successful 'I didn't know' defence was so rare it might well have made the *Guinness Book of Records* had it been offered for consideration.

So did this unusual verdict have more to do with business and diplomatic issues than justice? Hanging two Dutch citizens at roughly the same time, and one of them an older, middle-aged woman, could have meant an economic and diplomatic backlash from Holland. Mr Suppiah told me that he was able to persuade the judge that his client really didn't know she was in possession of a valuable consignment of heroin. But he added: 'There was a lot of sympathy for her and I don't think Singapore wanted to hang her. The authorities made sure she received a very fair trial. Everyone was relieved, of course, when she was freed.'

Judge Lai said at the end of the trial that he would produce a written judgment, but he did not do so. There was no appeal against his decision by the prosecution, either. Lawnet.com, the renowned international legal recording service, merely has the words 'No record' by Krol-Hmelak's name. There is also no trace of the court transcripts. It is as though someone wanted this case to vanish from the records. The only account of the trial is one that Mr Suppiah, Krol-Hmelak's lawyer, prepared himself and which he allowed me to copy. According to him, Judge Lai said in his summing up:

We have gone through 28 days of trial and at the appropriate time, I will be delivering a judgment in full, in writing. But very briefly, Mrs Krol, it is the finding of this court, having heard you under cross-examination, that more probably than not, you did not know that the pistons contained diamorphine. I believe you on your evidence when it comes to the crucial elements of the case. You have on occasions lied to the police officers, and even to this Court, but they did not undermine my belief in your evidence because your version was consistent from the beginning to the end in its essential element and you have discharged the burden of rebutting the evidence, the presumption against you. So you are acquitted of the charge and you may go free.

Then he asked Peter Johnson to stand up. Judge Lai took on a different tone. He said:

As for you, your evidence has been less satisfactory. Your different versions given to the CNB officers and your evidence in Court have shown that by nature you are quite a mendacious person. Between your evidence and that of Mrs Krol, I would accept her evidence rather than yours. Having said that, it is still the finding of this Court that it was Mrs Krol who handed you the piston ring. Mrs Krol said to this Court that you appeared surprised when she mentioned to you that Mr Oloo gave the piston to her in Bangkok. And it is her evidence, which I accept, that you collected the piston from her to go and find out about cargoeing. But for her evidence, I don't think you would have discharged your onus of proof. Mrs Krol has no reason to help you but she has given evidence which turned the case in your favour. I have therefore come to the conclusion that more probably than not, you also did not know that there was diamorphine in the pistons. You are also acquitted and discharged.

The DPP then asked, 'The exhibits, Your Honour?'

Judge Lai replied, 'The exhibits are to be returned to the accused persons and the drugs to be forfeited.'

While researching the background to this case, I had two long interviews with the renowned Mr P. Suppiah and his personal summing up of the trial was invaluable. During *my* trial in the Supreme Court, Mr Suppiah came to watch some of the proceedings. We discussed the case during the lunch break. He had just read the first edition of this book and said he had no complaints concerning my assertions concerning his client and Johnson. I was nevertheless found guilty of 'scandalising the judiciary' for saying that the verdict in Krol's and Johnson's case appeared to have been decided on political rather than judicial grounds. (Judge Lai died from stomach cancer in 2006 and so it is not possible to know what his reaction would have been to my case.)

Mr Suppiah's epilogue is apt. It said:

Under normal circumstances the First Accused must give evidence first who in this case was Peter Johnson. However, with leave of the Court, Maria Krol gave evidence first even though she was the Second Accused, followed by Johnson. The reason for this arrangement was to have a continuous picture of the events that took place, as it was Mrs Krol who brought the pistons from Bangkok to Singapore and gave one to Johnson. Nowhere in her evidence did Mrs Krol implicate him. She said Johnson did not know anything about the pistons and he was rather surprised when Mrs Krol told him about them. There has been unnecessary cross-examination of Mrs Krol by counsel for Johnson as can be seen from the trial notes. Why this was so it is difficult to fathom. The cross-examination was extensively towards attacking her credibility ... The joint trial in fact benefited Johnson, leading to his acquittal on Krol's evidence ... After Johnson was acquitted, the US$50,000 was returned to him. He wanted to give some to Mrs Krol to settle her outstanding hotel bill which she rejected. There has been no written judgment on the case and there was no appeal against the Judge's decision.

As soon as she was declared innocent, Krol-Hmelak wanted to leave for home immediately. A seat had been reserved for her on the evening KLM flight to Amsterdam. But a last-minute hitch brought new terror for her. All her friends and Dutch Embassy staff were waiting at Changi Airport to see her off. But instead she was reminded of a pending charge for the consumption of drugs, due to be heard at the lower court the next day. She was permitted to stay the night at a hotel instead of being returned to the prison cell. The next morning the Attorney-General formally withdrew the charge. Krol-Hmelak left for the Netherlands ten hours later. She has never returned to Singapore. The result, despite the uproar when Johannes van Damme was hanged, meant business as usual between the two countries. No one wanted another demand for Dutch warships to be sent to Singapore to spring this ageing woman from the shadow of the gallows.

11

DEAD WOMAN WALKING

'She went to the gallows dressed all in white. Not virginal white but, for hundreds of thousands of Filipinos, the white of innocence.' This is what one Filipino journalist wrote the day domestic worker Flor Contemplacion was hanged in Singapore. Many of her country-folk refused to believe she had committed the two murders she confessed to. Some maintain she was tortured to obtain the confession. Her execution produced howls of protest in the Philippines and sparked outrage among her fellow citizens in Singapore and around the world.

An estimated four million Filipinos, mainly young women, slave away in many foreign countries doing the kind of work no one else wants to do. The Philippine economy is heavily dependent on the money they send home; in the 1990s it was estimated to be more than US$2 billion annually. A former laundry worker, Flor Contemplacion was one of them.

Contemplacion first arrived in Singapore in 1988. She worked literally from dawn to midnight, keeping two households clean and caring for her employer's child seven days a week without any time off. On 4 May 1991, after getting up at 6 am to mop floors and wash her employer's car, she was allowed a rare moment off to visit another domestic worker, thirty-four-year-old Delia Maga. According to her confession, she wanted Delia to take a bag of personal items back to the Philippines for her family, but Delia refused, and Contemplacion, physically exhausted and emotionally drained, flew into an uncontrollable, maniacal rage.

It is unclear to this day exactly what happened, but Delia Maga was later found strangled to death. Delia had been charged with the care of her employer's four-year-old son, who was also found dead. It is commonly suggested that he was drowned in a bucket of water. After reading Maga's diary, police identified Flor Contemplacion as a possible suspect and, under interrogation, Contemplacion confessed to the murders of both Maga and the young boy.

When she was tried, Contemplacion again admitted to the killings, but no consideration as to her mental history or state of mind was given and she was sentenced to death. Pleading guilt was the strategy recommended by her court-appointed lawyer; it seems the aim was to win clemency when the case inevitably reached the Supreme Court, but it was a fatal error.

The case began in a low key and, as is the norm in Singapore, little was reported in the local media. Contemplacion was seen as just another lowly maid 'gone bad'. During the four years she was in jail and on death row, she was visited only nine times by staff from the Philippine consulate. Consequently, news of her plight took a long time to get back to the media in her own country. Back home in Manila, when journalists finally began reporting Contemplacion's tragic situation, it seemed to many that their own diplomats had abandoned this poor woman to her fate in a country she hardly knew, and as the execution date neared, Filipino citizens took to the streets. Many staged daily demonstrations outside Singapore embassies and consulates and took part in protest marches in Manila and other large cities. Senatorial and local elections were imminent and Philippines President Fidel Ramos found himself at the mercy of the voting masses. He tried to get tough and appealed to Singapore's then President Ong Teng Cheong for a reprieve. It was turned down. The Singapore media ignored the growing diplomatic rift.

Then new witnesses came forward; newspaper articles in the Philippines gave accounts of Contemplacion's treatment in Singapore at the hands of the police, saying she had been stripped naked and tortured until she confessed—yet no one could prove her innocence, and Contemplacion never withdrew her confession.

One late failed appeal said Contemplacion had suffered bouts of insanity as a child. Had this evidence been produced earlier it might have convinced government lawyers and psychiatrists she should not be hanged. It was obvious to everyone she'd had a serious mental breakdown. Even the police said she broke down under the unrelenting pressure of her work, from which she had little or no respite. 'She must have snapped,' wrote one investigating officer. But it made no difference. Once she had been tried and found guilty no further evidence was permitted to be introduced.

On the evening of Thursday, 16 March 1995, the day before Contemplacion's execution, thousands of her country-folk—mostly fellow maids and labourers—gathered in small groups across Singapore. To them it was like a death in the family or, as one Filipina journalist wrote, 'like a family member being murdered by a cold, soulless state called Singapore'. They held silent vigils as a prequel to a secret plan to converge on Changi Prison before dawn for a final, vociferous mass demonstration to show their horror and disgust at what was about to take place. 'Added to this was a repugnance of a Singapore justice system that, seen from the Philippines, was so haughty it was not prepared to admit a mistake had been made,' another journalist wrote at the time. Contemplacion's supporters set out by bus, train, taxi, motorbike, bicycle and on foot. But the plan leaked out. Roadblocks were put up on all routes leading to the prison near Changi village, machine-gun nests were installed on rooftops above the main entrance and Gurkha troops stood by ready for action.

For Darshan Singh, hanging a woman was no different from hanging a man. He was up bright and early the next morning, arriving at the prison in a chauffeured prison vehicle at 4 am. He was dressed casually as always—shorts, singlet and sandals—and he went about his business in his usual calm and methodical way. He had already made complete preparations according to the rules the day before. Contemplacion had been weighed and her physique judged so he could calculate how far she should drop. Being slightly built and not very tall, for her it would be a long drop. Singh had spoken to the condemned woman at length, trying to make her feel as relaxed as possible. He explained that he did not want to hang her; it was his job, and she had been sentenced by the court. That was none of his doing. He asked if she would like to donate her organs, saying that her life would not have been entirely worthless if she could save someone else, but when we spoke he told me it was so long ago he could not remember if she signed the consent document or not.

A final photograph of Contemplacion, wearing her best clothes, was taken for her family to remember her by. Singh assured her she would feel no pain; that it would be over in a split second. 'You don't want to spend the rest of your life in this terrible place,' he told her, as he had told so many others. 'That would be a living death, wouldn't it?'

It was nearing dawn. Just minutes away. He checked his watch, shackled her arms behind her back and led her to the final steps to the gallows. Once on the trap door, her legs were quickly strapped together. Then he uttered the words he first revealed to me in that memorable interview shortly before he hanged Nguyen Van Tuong: 'I am sending you to a better place than this.' Singh pulled the lever. The twin trap doors disappeared from under her feet. It was all over in a split second as he promised. Her neck broke where he calculated it would and her body was left to hang for ten to twenty minutes before being taken down. Shortly afterwards, Singh returned to his home in an official car with a cheque for his morning's work. It was $325—the rate that particular year.

The Philippines almost came to a complete standstill that day. The noise that boomed from almost every corner of the nation sounded more like drums of war. At a pre-arranged time, armed with hammers, clubs, pots and pans, musical instruments—anything with which to make deafening noises—Filipinos began the biggest civil protest ever seen in their country. School children of all ages took off their shoes in their classrooms and banged them against their desks. Housewives and factory workers picked up any object they could find to add to the din. Motorists honked their car horns and demonstrators carrying placards paraded outside the Singapore embassy in Manila to express their united horror at what had taken place on the gallows that morning. A Philippines citizen now working in Singapore told me: 'I was still in school when all this happened. Everyone was so angry that Flor was hanged. It was brutal. She should have been sent to a mental hospital instead of being killed. Everyone in my country remembers her name.'

This sense of outrage in Flor Contemplacion's home country brought the government to crisis point. The foreign affairs secretary resigned, then the labor secretary, admitting that they had failed in their duty of care to their citizens working overseas. President Ramos sacked the previous ambassador to Singapore and suspended the current ambassador, cancelling all trade and state visits.

Several movies were made, including *The Flor Contemplacion Story*, each claiming to tell the true story behind the tragic event. The movies were highly emotive, showing Contemplacion being drugged, denied food, water and the toilet, water-boarded, even molested by the Singapore police in a bid to extract a confession. I'm told that these films are still shown regularly on Filipino television.

It took a very long time for things to simmer down in Manila. President Ramos held an inquiry into the case and in 1996 ordered that Delia Maga's remains be exhumed to determine her cause of death. The conclusion was that Contemplacion probably was guilty, not withstanding the appalling conditions she worked under that drove her to madness, but many people in the Philippines believe to this day that she was innocent. President Ramos called her 'a heroine', and made sure that her dependent children were provided for.

One Manila journalist wrote: 'If there is a real story of Contemplacion, it is not that she did or did not kill two people in Singapore. It is that, in her death, she came to symbolise the millions of Filipinos driven by poverty to leave their families and take their chances abroad. Some are looked down on as little more than modern-day serfs; others are treated with dignity. But all are where they are because they have yet to benefit from Asia's prospering economies.'

The hanging of this disturbed woman still resonates across Southeast Asia to this day, but particularly in the Philippines. The diplomatic, finance and business meltdown between the two countries that followed her execution set the stage for Singapore never to hang another maid again. So it was quite a different story when another Filipino maid was arrested in Singapore in 2005 for what became known as 'The Body Parts Murder'.

12

THE MAID THEY COULD NOT HANG

When Filipina maid Guen Aguilar appeared in court on 15 September 2005 charged with one of the most gruesome murders in Singapore history, the diplomatic turn-out from her country's embassy astounded everyone. The ambassador, Belen Anota, flanked by top diplomatic officials and prominent members of the Filipino community, filed into the court room. Other Filipinos, mostly young domestic workers and labourers, packed the public gallery and stood in groups around the courthouse. Two of Manila's biggest television stations sent camera crews and another dozen print writers and photographers arrived to cover the proceedings. Their numbers were swelled by international wire services including AFP, AP, Reuters and representatives from the local media such as the *Straits Times*, *Today* and the *New Paper*.

Aguilar, a twenty-nine-year-old mother of two, was facing death by hanging for the murder of her close friend and neighbour Jane La Puebla, a fellow Filipina domestic worker from her home town. But if she were executed, it would be regarded in Manila and across the Filipino diaspora almost as an act of war—and Singapore knew it only too well. Although it was almost ten years since another Filipina maid had been hanged, everyone remembered her name: Flor Contemplacion. Her execution had sparked political upheaval in the Philippines and a huge diplomatic row with Singapore, still remembered to this day. Even when the atmosphere thawed things were never quite the same again. Bilateral ties had since been normalised and Singapore was once again a major investor in the Philippines, but there would always be a bitter taste in the mouths of many Filipinos.

Aguilar was a hard-working wife who grew up as an orphan, the third among five siblings. She was in her second year studying Hotel and Restaurant Management at the University of Baguio when she went to work abroad. Aguilar's two sons, Mark, seven, and Edwin, six, were at home in the Philippines with their father, Edwin, a farm hand. They had not seen their mother since August 2002 when she left to work as a maid in Singapore. They were hoping she would be home for Christmas—just as she had promised in her last text message just after 7 pm on Friday 9 September, the very night Singaporeans were learning of the gruesome killing on the television.

The hunt for the killer began when dismembered parts of a woman's body were found in various parts of the city. Arms and legs were found in bags in and around an Orchard Road shopping centre. Then a woman's partly clad torso was found at MacRitchie Reservoir, a spot popular with joggers, picnickers and tourists. Not long after, police seized a cleaver at the premises where Aguilar worked. They also took possession of CCTV video footage showing the two women together shortly before La Puebla's death. Forensic evidence connected the dots. There was plenty of blood to work with.

The police in Singapore hold suspects without access to counsel while investigations are still underway—something that does not happen in the Philippines. This caused consternation among legal advisers in Manila. They recalled what had happened to Contemplacion, who was interrogated for days and quickly confessed to the crimes. More ominous for Aguilar was the fact that the Singaporean justice system doesn't consider insanity grounds for acquittal. Even though she was examined by psychiatrists who said she was mentally unbalanced at the time of the murders, she could still have received the death penalty. I found from my searches of court records that such cases are not unusual in Singapore.

Back home in the Philippines, the story made garish headlines, but this time the government took immediate action, appealing to its media to stop sensational reporting. 'We don't want a repeat of the Flor Contemplacion furore,' Justice Secretary Raul Gonzalez told the *Straits Times*. Haunted and shamed by that case, the Philippine government was generous in its support for both the La Puebla and Aguilar families. Miriam Cuasay, Manila's labour attaché in Singapore, immediately assigned Maria Isleta as Aguilar's Philippine legal counsel. Labor Secretary Patricia Tomas promised to provide financial assistance to the family of the victim.

In Singapore, Ambassador Anota issued press reports from his embassy every few days. The message from Manila was clear: everyone from the president down was determined that Aguilar should have a fair trial and would not be cast aside and executed by Singapore as just another 'havoc maid'. They would be watching every aspect of the police investigation and trial very closely. The large contingent from the Philippines embassy who turned out for Aguilar's initial hearing, including the ambassador himself, was proof of that—and when Aguilar first saw her husband Edwin, flanked by her fellow citizens, standing shoulder to shoulder with them inside the court room, she broke into tears. All this attention to Aguilar's welfare was a far cry from the way Flor Contemplacion was treated—virtually ignored by her embassy until it was too late for any kind of government intervention or support.

Singapore officials also issued regular updates to the media, and permitted Aguilar's husband to see her in her cell—something almost unheard of in Singapore while a serious case like this was still under investigation. For someone who had allegedly committed such a gruesome crime, Guen Aguilar was being treated with kid gloves. Officials even invited coroner's examiners from the Philippines to perform a joint autopsy on the deceased, to avoid any possible accusations of a frame-up, and the Philippines National Bureau of

Investigation sent pathologists Cesar Bisquera and Raquel Fortun along to observe.

Many Filipinos did in fact suspect that Aguilar might have been framed, refusing to believe that she could have committed such a gruesome crime. Chopping with a meat cleaver through raw tendon, sinew and bone to decapitate a woman's head and limbs would require brute strength, the theory went—and depositing these body parts in very public places did not seem to be an intelligent act, unless one wanted them to be found easily. It was tempting for Filipinos to conclude that Aguilar was a convenient scapegoat for someone else's crime.

Every observer of the case waited anxiously for the verdict. It came on 29 May 2006. To everyone's relief Aguilar was jailed for ten years, after the court reduced the charges from murder to manslaughter. Exactly why the young woman killed her friend was never established. Unconfirmed reports said it was over a love triangle with a Singapore taxi driver, but evidence was produced during the trial suggested that she was mentally unsound and had killed La Puebla because of a money dispute. 'Her illness did not in any way dispossess her of that ability to distinguish between right and wrong,' said High Court Judge V.K. Rajah. 'Upon taking all the relevant circumstances, I determine that the appropriate sentence for the accused is a term of imprisonment of ten years.'

Aguilar, wearing an orange prison suit, was expressionless when the sentence was read out. Her husband Edwin and sister were in the court along with Philippine embassy officials. Even the mayor of her home town arrived to give his support. 'We are happy with the sentencing,' said her lawyer Sashi Nathan. 'Earlier there were some concerns that she might get a life sentence, so this is a huge relief for Guen.'

It was also a huge relief for Singapore. Of course, they knew they could not hang her. Flor Contemplacion's death on the gallows, it seems, was not entirely in vain. In this way her case reminded me of that of another deranged young woman, Ruth Ellis, the last woman ever hanged in England. Ellis went to the gallows after shooting her lover in a moment of madness. Her execution ignited fierce opposition to the death penalty in Britain and became one more nail in the coffin of capital punishment. Not long afterwards, capital punishment was abolished there for all time.

After Guen Aguilar's case was over, a Singapore lawyer told me: 'I am prepared to bet everything I own they will never hang another maid in this country again.'

13

LICENSED TO KILL?

For several weeks in July 2004—shortly before Australian drug trafficker Nguyen Van Tuong's appeal against the death penalty was to be heard—dozens of people took to the streets of Jakarta to make vociferous, banner-waving protests outside the Singapore embassy. But this was not a prelude to the fight to save Nguyen from the hangman. They were members of the Working Forum on Justice and they were demanding the abolition of the death penalty for domestic helpers and other migrant workers in Singapore. 'We have also launched worldwide actions to take our protest to the International Labour Organization,' said Anis Hidayah, an activist from Migrant Care who coordinated the protest. The protesters also demanded that Singapore, Indonesia and Malaysia ratify the international law to protect migrant workers' human rights. Migrant workers face horrendous conditions all over the world but particularly in such places as the Middle East and, more importantly at this time, Singapore.

'Uniquely Singapore' is a slogan carefully crafted for the tourism industry. But following a spate of grisly murders by maids of their employers, this image was being overshadowed by a new slogan, 'Maid In Singapore'. There happened to be five Indonesian maids awaiting trial for the murders of their Singaporean employers. Four of them faced the death penalty. The cases had highlighted the stressful working conditions of many foreign domestic workers, often at the hands of abusive employers. Many are forced to work long days without even a single day off year in and year out. Like the Filipinas Flor Contemplacion and Guen Aguilar, the five young Indonesians had cracked under the strain, committing gruesome murders that stunned Singapore, especially its government. If they had to hang any of these women, some barely out of their teens, the uproar around the world, particularly in their homeland—a vital economic partner in ASEAN—would be catastrophic. Everyone recalled the diplomatic and economic meltdown that occurred when Flor Contemplacion was hanged in 1995.

As well as demanding the end of the death penalty for maids, the demonstrators in Jakarta also demanded the eradication of any form of physical, mental or sexual abuse directed against domestic helpers and migrant workers, with hefty punishments for the perpetrators. 'The crimes committed by migrant workers are a reaction to the accumulation of resentment against unjust and brutal treatment by their employers,' said Anis Hidayah.

At another protest in front of the Singapore embassy a week later, these human rights activists were received by the First Secretary. The ambassador could not see them because he was on leave, they were told. 'The embassy official did speak to us,' Hidayah told journalists later. 'During the meeting they explained they could not do anything to stop the death penalty in Singapore. It was a matter for the courts.' The protesters, wearing black sacks on their heads as a symbol of people awaiting execution, declared they would continue their efforts to have the death penalty scrapped in Singapore. One of their black banners demanded 'Free Our Foreign Exchange-Earning Heroes' and another 'Stop Women and Child Trafficking'. The embassy official promised their demands would be conveyed to the government in Singapore.

A few months earlier, in April 2004, a delegation of Indonesian NGOs had travelled to the United Nations Human Rights High

Commission in Geneva to raise the issue of this threat of the death sentence. In early May 2004 the Indonesian Minister for Women's Empowerment and the Minister of Manpower and Transmigration went to visit the five accused in Changi Prison. 'Unfortunately,' wrote the Indonesian campaigner Wahyu Susilo of Migrant Care, 'the Singapore government refused them permission to visit these distressed young women facing the death penalty.' This further angered the activists and government officials. Migrant Care continued their campaign, demanding that the Indonesian government concentrate on legal efforts and political diplomacy to free these workers from the death penalty on grounds that it was a violation of human rights. Wahyu Susilo added: 'If the Indonesian government does demand that Singapore remove the possibility of a death sentence for the five women, then it will also have to review the death penalty in our own criminal law system. More importantly, the government should immediately enact legislation to protect migrant workers. This legislation should concentrate on females working overseas, since this group is particularly vulnerable to violence.'

In the first murder trial, two Indonesian maids, one known only as Juminem, aged eighteen, and her close friend Siti Aminah, aged fifteen, were jointly charged with murder. The two had moved from East Java to Singapore and began working for Esther Ang and her ex-husband. Juminem was Ang's maid and Siti worked for her ex-husband in a separate but nearby household. The two maids were said to be very close and not to have had any other friends. Since their employers, although divorced, remained on good terms the girls saw each other regularly. But relations between Juminem and Ang were not happy. On 2 March 2004 the two maids took turns to suffocate Ang with a pillow and beat her about the head and stomach with a wine bottle at her home. The pair then faked a break-in by taking Ang's money and valuables. Juminem then forged her employer's signature on a cheque for S$25,000 payable to Siti Aminah. It was revealed in court documents that Juminem had first planned to kill Ang about a week earlier because she was 'unreasonable and oppressive', and enlisted the help of Siti. Justice Choo Han Teck found that Juminem had been suffering from 'reactive depression' as a result of loneliness, financial worry and her employer's demands. The defence had quoted extensively from her diary, illustrating the way her mood had changed over the previous months. She was found guilty of culpable homicide not amounting to murder and sentenced to life imprisonment instead of ending up on the scaffold. As for Siti Aminah, the court found that she had been under 'severe stress', particularly from her employer's elderly mother who had called her names and pushed her around. She was only fifteen and of borderline intelligence. The judge said she was easily led by others, especially her best friend. She was sentenced to ten years' jail.

Severe though those sentences were, everyone heaved a sigh of relief. Siti could not have been hanged anyway because of her age, but if that had been Juminem's fate the reaction in other parts of Asia would have been disastrous for both countries, but especially Singapore. The demonstration outside the Singapore Embassy in Jakarta a few months earlier had been warning enough. With relations between Indonesia and Singapore often on a knife edge, many observers felt that the risk of a diplomatic row, an economic meltdown and a threatened ban on sending maids to Singapore may have impinged on the verdicts. The judgment offered little comfort to the murdered woman's family, however. Her daughter told reporters that time had helped in the healing process but they had yet to obtain closure. After the case, the Indonesian Ambassador to Singapore, Mochamad Slamet Hidayat, said he was relieved at the verdict and that his embassy was working with Singapore's Ministry of Manpower—the government department that issues work permits—to strengthen cooperation.

The question of how a fifteen-year-old girl could obtain such a job in Singapore was also highlighted by the activists. 'It amounts to child trafficking and slave labour,' said Anis Hidayah. 'She was just a child at the time. She should have been in school. Now she is in prison. For ten years!' In a media release, Ambassador Hidayat commented: 'We will try to improve the quality of the domestic workers looking for employment in Singapore but at the same time we also appeal to employers in Singapore to treat our domestic workers humanely.'

The next maid to beat the noose was Sundarti Supriyanto, aged twenty-three. She was charged with murdering her abusive employer, Angie Ng, thirty-three, and her three-year-old daughter, Crystal, in May 2002. Supriyanto faced two mandatory death sentences. The circumstances of the crimes were horrific. She was accused of stabbing Angie Ng to death then setting the home alight with petrol. The little girl was burned to death.

While Justice M.P.H. Rubin found Supriyanto guilty, he convicted her on the lesser charge of culpable homicide or manslaughter after taking into account the 'ill-treatment' Ng had subjected her to. In fact, because the judiciary has no discretion in mandatory death sentence cases, the charges were reduced by the Attorney-General even before the trial began.

'This is an exceptionally tragic case. It is tragic and sad both for the deceased and the accused,' Rubin said before sentencing Supriyanto to life behind bars. He had rejected the prosecution's claim that Supriyanto was a 'cold-blooded killer' who carried out a 'mindless killing'. 'Despite all the lies uttered by the accused to extricate herself from her guilt, there was cogent evidence to conclude that the deceased subjected her to some measure of ill-treatment. In my view the cord of reason suddenly snapped when the accused could no longer control her emotions of feeling and despair'. The judge also referred to Ng depriving Supriyanto of food, then forcing the starving woman to accept biscuits from other people who pretended to pity her. This amounted to physical and mental ill-treatment, the judge said. Many saw this as yet another case of an unofficial moratorium being put on the death penalty where maids who murder their employees and members of their families were concerned.

In July 2005, a young Indonesian maid known only as Rohana appeared in the dock in the High Court charged with murdering her employer Tan Chiang Eng. She, too, was facing the death penalty. But she also managed to dodge the noose—as horrible as the nature of the killing was.

Shortly before the trial began on 5 July 2005, the Indonesian news agency issued a report that the government had sent a team of lawyers to Singapore to help defend their young citizen. The Indonesian government also escorted the girl's parents to Singapore to give her moral support. 'We hope the Singaporean court could be fair in handling this case,' a government spokesman said before the trial began.

Court documents show that Tan had been 'bashed on the head repeatedly' with a 10.5-kilogram amethyst ornament, the sort that adorns many Chinese living rooms for good luck. Then she was throttled to death. She had seventy-five wounds in total, including fourteen to her head. She was missing two front teeth, had a deep cut over her right eyebrow and a fractured right eye socket. But it was clear the divorced mother of two put up a fight when Rohana, then twenty, first bludgeoned her with the ornament after being scolded for oversleeping. Bleeding from the forehead, Tan made her way to the living room, calling for her twelve-year-old daughter, who was sleeping with her younger sister, six, in the master bedroom. Fearing the girls would wake up, Rohana picked up the stone ornament and again brought it down on Tan's head so hard that it broke in pieces.

A full account was given in court of what happened next: 'She covered Madam Tan's mouth with her hand to stop her from screaming but was bitten and kicked. She next picked up a piece of the stone and brought it down on Madam Tan's face once more. Then she started strangling the bleeding woman with her bare hands.' That was when the doorbell rang. To stop people hearing her boss's cries, Rohana dragged her by the hair into the toilet adjoining the kitchen, banging her head on the wall and on the floor repeatedly. Tan continued to scream and to plead for her life, saying that her daughters needed her. Unmoved, Rohana dragged her into the storeroom.

'Ana, sorry lah,' pleaded Tan in Singlish.

'Like that already you say sorry,' Rohana replied.

'Ana, let me talk first,' said Tan.

'No', was the reply. Then Rohana choked the life out of her.

Although the public prosecutor demanded Rohana should be jailed for life, the judge sentenced her to only ten years instead. Had this murder occurred before Flor Contemplacion was hanged, Rohana would without doubt have gone to the gallows.

Yet another sensational murder was revealed when an Indonesian maid strangled her employer's mother-in-law, then slit her wrist to make it look like suicide. Purwanti Parji, nineteen, described as another 'havoc maid' by the local media, was jailed for life. She had killed her employer, Har Chit Heang, fifty-seven, in her Tai Keng Gardens home on 4 August 2004, because she had been 'too harsh' with her. The case was heard by Judicial Commissioner V.K. Rajah, who said that the 'callous and heinous crime' could be neither justified nor condoned as a response to 'maid abuse'. It was clear, he said, that she had not acted because of some grave and sudden or physical provocation, and she had tried systematically to cover up her involvement in the killing, which showed that she had thought through the consequences of her 'diabolical act'. Like violent and abusive employers, domestic workers who resort to violence in retaliation should expect harsh sentences, he added.

Though initially charged with murder, Purwanti pleaded guilty to a reduced charge of manslaughter. But had she been found guilty of murder, being under the age of eighteen at the time of the crime, she would not have been sent to the gallows anyway. In court, Purwanti apologised to the victim's family, saying she was very remorseful for what she had done. But the family refused to accept it. Har's older son, Leong Meng Wei, thirty-three, said that the killing was a 'stupid act'. Meanwhile, Har's husband, Michael Leong Kit Heang, fifty-eight, a businessman, told local reporters after the case that while Purwanti may have escaped the death penalty, the sentence was a firm and fair one. 'She's a dangerous person,' he said.

In mitigation, her assigned lawyer, Subhas Anandan, together with Mohamed Nasser Mohamed Ismail, said that Har had constantly nagged and cursed the young girl. Purwanti, who had to care for her three step-brothers from the age of nine, found herself working for two households when she came to Singapore to work in November 2002—in Tai Keng Gardens and at Har's daughter-in-law's home in Woodlands. Har also deprived her of food and would scold her for eating more than she thought she should, said the lawyer. She was often given bread to eat by the maid next door. That morning, Har had scolded Purwanti for not cleaning the toilet properly and tried to slap her. 'That was the final straw,' said Anandan. Purwanti snapped and decided to kill her tormentor. 'If maids are not treated well, unexpected and unpleasant consequences may arise' said Anandan, who urged the court not to impose life imprisonment on Purwanti, a first-time offender. However, the judge said that she was 'no shrinking violet unable to fend for herself' or to communicate her difficulties or distress to the world at large. She had killed Har because of long-standing resentment. It was, he said, a 'disturbing case' with a number of aggravating features. Arguing for a life sentence, Deputy Public Prosecutor Jaswant Singh said the killing was deliberate and calculated, not due to any momentary loss of self-control or sudden rage but motivated by ill-feeling. Purwanti was no simpleton. She even cut her own fingernails when she saw the marks left on the neck of the deceased, he said.

Purwanti was one of a string of Indonesian maids who had committed crimes that would ordinarily have attracted the death penalty that year. When these cases began coming to light, some activists began asking why, and discovered that Singapore's modern and up-to-date society relied on the labour of unwilling 'slaves', forced to work up to eighteen hours a day for years without ever getting a day off. Depending on their knowledge of English they would be paid from S$170 to S$350 per month, a pittance by Singapore standards. And most of that would be sent home to support their poverty-stricken families. Their duties included shopping, cooking, scrubbing, cleaning cars, washing, ironing and, more dangerously, cleaning the windows in their employers' high-rise apartments so they always sparkled inside and out.

Domestic workers often face poor working conditions, known as the three Ds—dirty, dangerous, difficult—and without any kind of normal legal recognition as workers, let alone human beings. Maltreatment by their employers includes violence, sexual abuse or even rape. Sometimes employers do not even pay them. They often work without safety equipment. Since 1999, more than 140 Indonesian domestic workers have died in workplace accidents, mostly as a result of falling from windows while cleaning them. Unlike other workers in Singapore, their conditions are not guaranteed under an employment act.

Only after the stories of the so-called 'havoc maids' got everyone's attention did the government pass a law that every maid should get one day off per month. But this is not compulsory, provided they are paid if they work on their official day off. On May Day 2008 all three local government-controlled newspapers, the *Straits Times*, the *New Paper* and *My Paper*, carried short articles arguing that by law maids should get one day off a week like everyone else. But the suggestion was greeted with disdain by many citizens, who responded that this would put an 'unfair burden' on employers. If it has taken more than forty years since independence to achieve the right to one day off a month for domestic workers, achieving the right to one day off a *week* seems like an impossible dream.

Adding to the pressure of inordinately long working hours, many Singaporean households have installed webcams or CCTV cameras that follow their maids virtually wherever they go. This is to ensure the maids do not get up to any kind of mischief while their employers are at work or enjoying themselves away from home.

Alex Au notes: 'One cannot deny some need to protect their homes and children, but webcams are merely treating the symptoms.' He says too many maids are still in their teens when they come to Singapore from rural villages.

> They have never been away from their families, and then suddenly they are contracted here for two years without a vacation. It's an emotional shock, they can't get the food they're used to, they miss their friends and they get homesick very easily ... They have had very little schooling and no awareness that cultures can be different ... There can be an infinite number of ways for misunderstanding and friction to arise. This then leads to the feeling of victimisation on the maid's part [which makes] conflict inevitable. Trying hard to keep the lid on the maids by locking them in the house, perhaps even under constant surveillance, doesn't solve the problem, but more likely piles on the pressure.

Au then poses the question:

> Has anyone made the connection between this state of affairs and the steady diet of news about maids murdering their employers and family members? In contrast, I can't recall a single instance of a foreign worker employed in the manufacturing, cleaning or construction industry—predominantly men from India, China, Bangladesh, Thailand and Burma—taking out their frustrations against their employers to the point of killing them! Does this have to do with the fact that cleaning and construction workers get days off? And that they have their own quarters to retire to, unlike domestic maids who have to live under their employer's roof and are under CCTV watch all the time? ... I am embarrassed that we have become a society so marked by inhumanity, I am embarrassed that we have a government that, far from providing moral leadership, has created a climate for inhumanity to metastasise like cancer. And it now seems maids have a licence to kill!

14

HER NAME WAS ANGEL

The sad story of Angel Mou Pui-Peng is all too familiar—a teenage girl who gets pregnant at sixteen is forced to leave her neighbourhood out of shame and inevitably drifts into poverty and petty crime to survive. She becomes an easy target for exploitation by more sophisticated people who make a fortune from drugs and do not care who suffers along the way.

Mou was a twenty-five-year-old single mother, originally from the then Portuguese province of Macau, but living in Hong Kong. She was arrested at Singapore's Changi Airport on 29 August 1991 with a suitcase containing twenty packets filled with 4.1 kilograms of heroin, according to the Central Narcotics Bureau. She had flown to Singapore from Bangkok. At her trial she claimed she did not know the false-bottomed suitcase contained the drug. She thought she was carrying contraband watches given to her by a couple she met by chance. There was no evidence that the syndicate involved in the run had been traced and arrested, or if there had been any serious attempts to track them down using intelligence she might well have provided. And, as usual in Singapore, her appeals were rejected out of hand. No one was prepared to consider that she might well have been hoodwinked and was telling the truth. In fact, there was no evidence to suggest she was or wasn't innocent of trafficking drugs; having them in her possession was all the system wanted to know.

But if the Lion City shows no conscience or fear hanging women for drug offences or murder—unless a major foreign power is twisting its economic tail—it does sometimes, just occasionally, show a glimmer of humanity. A rare, surprise gesture of 'kindness', as it was described at the time, came shortly before Mou's scheduled execution on 22 December 1994.

Because it was Christmas, she was granted a temporary stay of execution after a plea by her mother and nine-year-old son. Mou was originally scheduled to hang simultaneously with two Singaporean drug traffickers who were not Christians. The authorities bent the rules and allowed her devout Christian family to visit her in Changi Prison every day during the entire religious season. They then deemed that the young woman's life should come to an end just as the sun rose on the twelfth day of Christmas, Friday 6 January 1995. They could not put it off any longer.

Singapore's chief executioner Darshan Singh told me about Mou's execution. At about 5.50 am, Singh entered the young woman's cell to prepare her. After talking gently to her, he pinioned her arms behind her back and secured them with handcuffs. Then he walked her into the death chamber. Mou, a slim woman barely 5 feet tall, was calm and resigned to her fate, her lawyer said later. Singh checked his watch. The noose was quickly positioned around her slender neck. Then, like a magician, he produced a white linen cap and placed it over her head in one deft movement. Before he pulled the lever he uttered the same words he said every time he hanged someone: 'I am sending you to a better place than this.' Mou was gone. To a better place? Being a Christian, perhaps she believed this.

After the execution her body was returned to relatives to be cremated that evening at Mount Vernon Crematorium. There was a short service for family and friends. 'Our sister Mou has now been taken to heaven—a place we will go and we shall hope to see her there one day', an elderly pastor, speaking in Cantonese, told the congregation of some twenty-five people. 'When are you coming back to Hong Kong?' one young distressed woman cried, unable to comprehend what had happened. Mou's sister Cecilia and a few others dared to watch as the coffin, covered in black velvet, disappeared into the furnace. Her father, reportedly reconciled with his daughter during her brief stay of execution, broke down uncontrollably after the cremation.

In Lisbon, President Mario Soares and the Portuguese government had appealed for clemency on the grounds of Mou's youth and the fact that she was only a low-level carrier. But according to officials in Portugal, Singapore responded that it could not differentiate between foreigners and its own people. The Governor of Macau, Rocha Viera Vasco, said he was supported by the people of the Portuguese province in expressing deep sorrow over Mou's execution and criticised Singapore's judicial system. 'For someone like me who is a citizen of a country that takes pride as one of the first to abolish capital punishment, her loss by execution is incomprehensible and even revolting,' he said. Chris Patten, Hong Kong's Governor at the time, said the British colony had supported a plea for clemency put forward by Britain and the European Union. Of course, Singapore was determined not to lose face. Mou's lawyer, Peter Yap, told a Hong Kong newspaper she was 'normal and calm' when he last saw her. He said she 'was emotionally stable and prepared to die. Spiritually she is very strong.' He also said Mou was comforted by the settlement of guardianship for her son. A commentary published on capitalpunishmentuk.org after Mou was hanged said:

Sadly she was sent as a carrier to one of the few countries in the world where they have no compunction about executing young women. Whilst I accept that she was guilty, I doubt somehow that she was evil but rather think her motive was purely the small sum she hoped to make had she got away with it. Interestingly most Singaporeans support their tough laws and executions rate just a paragraph or two in the press, if mentioned at all. Why is it that even in countries like

Singapore and Malaysia people are still not deterred from crime by the death penalty? Are they stupid, desperate for money or do they think that somehow they won't be caught? Mou may or may not have known what she was carrying, but even if you believe her story, she knew she was smuggling which, no doubt, would have carried a heavy prison sentence in Singapore.

What puzzled me while carrying out research for this book was that nothing is ever heard about the syndicates who entice these mules into their orbit, often by trickery, then warn them of the dire consequences if they try to back out. The only way out, they are told, is feet first! If the Singapore authorities can send a silly young single mother like Mou to her death on the gallows why not use her instead as bait—whether she knows it or not—to trace and hook her handlers at both ends of the drug run? Instead of being hanged, she could have become a useful tool in the fight against the big-time traffickers. When I raised this question with an expert in the field he simply replied that the world of drug cartels is far murkier than anyone could possibly imagine.

The year 1995 was one of the busiest on the gallows in Singapore. According to Amnesty International more than fifty people were hanged in Singapore that year, the majority for drug offences. On 27 September 1996 six people were hanged in one morning, three at a time. Four more had been hanged the previous Friday, all for drug trafficking. It is believed that the current rate of executions remains high, but as official figures are no longer released publicly, it is impossible to confirm exactly how many people are hanged in Singapore each year.

15

THE FAVOURED FEW

It's Friday night. The rich and privileged are iced up, dancing wildly to the thumping beat of techno music. They have popped a pill or two, eased down with vintage champagne, and they are having a whale of a time. It was very likely one of those Friday nights after a Friday morning when a hapless mule—one who possibly provided the cocaine they'd just stuck up their noses—had been dancing, too. But for him or her it was no fun. Their jerky moves were on the end of a rope. But eighteen hours or so later, the revellers, like the majority of the population, would not know or care who had been hanged. Little news of what goes on behind Changi Prison's grim walls ever gets out.

These glamorous young things are in a drug-hazed here-and-now world, bent on enjoying themselves as intensely as possible. As members of Singapore's so-called high society—often the privileged and pampered sons and daughters of Singapore's elite, the newest batch of production-line tycoons or expensive foreign talent and entrepreneurs from Australia, Britain, the US or Germany—they are the ones who get photographed for the celebrity gossip columns. They see themselves as invincible and beyond the law. During the small hours, when the nightspots around Boat Quay and Clarke Quay are closing, they jump into limos to be whisked away to house parties where the cocaine is just as plentiful.

The surprise roundup began on 7 October 2004. It was a lengthy investigation. Those arrested—sixteen Singaporeans and seven foreigners, including two permanent residents—were from the upper classes, and included brokers, executives and an award-winning French chef. Of the arrests that night, the most surprising was that of thirty-five-year-old Dinesh Singh Bhatia, a private equity investor and the son of former High Court judge Amarjeet Singh. As a first offender Bhatia was facing a jail sentence of up to eighteen months and a heavy fine or both for consuming cocaine obtained from his close friend and supplier, Tunisian citizen Guiga Lyes Ben Laroussi. Instead, Bhatia was jailed for twelve months. According to his legal representative, People's Action Party MP K. Shanmugam—now Minister for Law—Bhatia was not an addict. He had been given the drug by a friend. Though he had a 'fleeting suspicion' the substance could be illegal, he took it on impulse, but 'did not know that it was cocaine.'

So should Bhatia, a sophisticate about town, have known he was snorting something illegal? On 7 April 2005, according to court records, Bhatia appealed against his jail sentence and asked for a heavy fine instead. Calling the previous sentence 'excessive', the Appeal Judge, V.K. Rajah, said that the district judge erred by not tailoring the sentence to fit the offender and failed to 'attach adequate weight and merit to all the relevant mitigating factors'. He said the trial judge did not adequately consider the fact that Bhatia's consumption was neither planned nor purchased. Justice Rajah then cut Bhatia's sentence to eight months. On 7 July 2005, the *Straits Times* reported that Bhatia was 'now at home serving out his sentence wearing an electronic tag he cannot remove'. It did not say when this more comfortable part of the sentence began.

At the time of the arrests a writer at the *New Paper* bravely commented: 'They live a lie. These are people on the move—young, urban and upwardly mobile professionals. At night they drive flashy cars and hit the expensive restaurants. This is the illicit cocaine party crowd right here in squeaky-clean Singapore.' Veteran journalist Seah Chiang Nee wrote a piece for the *Sunday Star* in which he quoted contributors to online chatrooms, who seemed manifestly unsympathetic, saying things such as: 'Only someone with a brain the size of a pea wouldn't know the consequences of doing drugs in Singapore,' or 'Cocaine is nature's way of telling you that you are making too much money.'

British expat Andrew Veale, a top financial broker and a ten-year resident, and his Singaporean girlfriend, Penelope Pang Su-yin, thirty-five, daughter of the organiser of the Miss Universe pageant, were next to appear in court. They too got off lightly with jail sentences amounting to no more than eight months with remission. They could have got eighteen months as first offenders. Veale worked in high finance and successfully appealed against deportation, despite the seriousness of his crime. Had he been a humble labourer from Bangladesh who overstayed his visa, he might well have been thrashed with the rattan cane, jailed and summarily deported.

Next in the dock was Nigel Simmonds. Wearing a dark suit, the bald, bespectacled Briton kept his head bowed throughout. He was accompanied in court by his brother and Japanese wife. Although Simmonds, forty, confessed to being a drug addict, his lawyers, Shashi Nathan and Peter Chean, tried to distinguish their client from the rest of the pack. He never took part in 'drug parties' allegedly organised by his supplier, Guiga, who had mysteriously managed to slip out of the country while on bail after his arrest. In fact, Nathan said, the Briton 'always made a conscious effort to stay away' from these functions. 'He did not know any of the other thirteen suspects well.' As for Guiga, he knew him only as 'the Arab'. Nathan said he was worried the arrests of many high-profile personalities gave the impression that all of them took drugs at private parties. But Simmonds was a loner, he said, who took drugs in solitude. 'He is an addict but not a member of these drug parties. He was so ashamed of his addiction that he had to hide it from his own wife.'

Nathan also submitted a psychiatric report by Dr Lim Yun Chin of Raffles Hospital documenting Simmonds' 'tumultuous childhood and youth'. He grew up in Malaysia, where his father, an army officer, was posted. Lim said in his report: 'It is not surprising that drugs and alcohol were the only way he knew how to cope.' The psychiatrist added that Simmonds had tried to use his talent and ability to lead a normal life but he kept meeting misfortunes which 'aggravated' his drug use. His wife lost a baby the previous year due to medical complications. Then his father died of stomach cancer a few months later. The economic downturn also made his job more stressful. 'He had no chance to escape from the scourge of addiction because of his rollercoaster emotional experience,' wrote Lim. Simmonds started psychiatric and counselling sessions after he was arrested and attended Narcotics Anonymous meetings. District Judge F.G. Remedios noted that the standard minimal sentence imposed on first-time drug offenders was twelve months. 'There are no circumstances in this case warranting a higher or lower sentence,' said the judge. Simmonds now edits a glossy magazine in Bali.

Dutchman Petrus van Wanrooij, managing director of Aspen Oil Broking, was also caught in the same swoop and jailed for eleven months for popping ecstasy pills. At fifty-seven, he was the oldest of the group picked up in the October 2004 bust. Wanrooij was arrested in his home during simultaneous raids all over the island. His excuse was perhaps the most original, even amusing. He admitted buying two tablets for S$60 to help correct an erectile dysfunction problem which he claimed Viagra could not fix. He bought the tablets from a man he knew as 'Tunis', later established to be Guiga, the leader of the drug syndicate.

Another favoured member of the high society circle who dodged the noose was No. 2 kingpin trafficker Marx Oh Wee Chee, a thirty-one-year-old owner of Zero Events Concepts and part-time disc jockey. All this put him in a perfect position as Guiga's sidekick.

Oh was arrested at his posh Hyde Park Gate home in Seletar in the surprise roundup and in April 2005 was jailed for six years and ordered to be given five strokes of the cane. He could have got twenty to thirty years' jail and fifteen strokes. Oh was originally found with 21.67 grams of cocaine—a mandatory hanging offence. Lucky Oh was given a discharge not amounting to an acquittal for this and another trafficking charge. The official line was that he had escaped the gallows because Guiga managed to flee from Singapore. It meant the prosecution had lost a potential prosecution witness. It all seemed so cosily convenient. To avoid any kind of accusations of favouritism for these chosen few, the authorities explained that if Guiga was ever arrested and brought back to Singapore, Oh might still be charged with the capital offence and hanged. But this seems very unlikely—he left Singapore soon after his release from Changi Prison and is now in business as a DJ in Kuala Lumpur, Malaysia.

Oh's luck was still in at the time of his trial, when he was given the minimum five years' jail and five strokes of the cane on one charge of trafficking in 0.56 grams of cannabis mixture. As far as the authorities were concerned, the sentencing of Oh, the only one convicted of trafficking, brought this particular scandal to a relatively happy, low-key end—despite having tarnished Singapore's drug-free image.

Apart from Guiga, another permanent resident, Sri Lankan Jeremy Shanmugam, forty, facing a two-year sentence, also managed to flee Singapore while on bail—several weeks ahead of Guiga. Award-winning chef François Mermilliod, to whom Nigel Simmonds gave a glowing write-up in the high-society magazine the *Tatler*, was luckier. Mermilliod, twenty-nine, who worked at a well-known Singapore restaurant, had been charged with possessing 0.5 grams of cocaine. He had called Guiga on that fatal day for a 'fix' and was roped in to receive a twelve months prison sentence, of which he served eight—two of them while wearing a bracelet to enable him to go back to work. More surprisingly, Mermilliod won his appeal against deportation partly on the grounds that he had contributed greatly to the food culture of Singapore, he told me. Mermilliod is now the owner of a high-end restaurant called Absinthe, close to the Central Narcotics Bureau HQ, and zips around town in a brand new Alfa Romeo.

Out of twenty-three people nabbed, fourteen were hauled to court. Noor Ashikin Abdul Aziz, the creative director of an advertising agency, and shipping firm boss Andy Ng Kwang Thiam, were both jailed for eleven months. Later, Anandan, who acted for five of the accused, solemnly told the *Straits Times*: 'The courts have driven home the point that there's no group of people that will be spared or given special treatment. Whether you are rich or the elite, the law will come down hard on you,' he said. 'If you are caught, you are dead meat.' Meanwhile, not having high-level connections or powerful governments willing and able to fight for them, Vignes Mourthi, Yen May Woen, Amara Tochi, Nguyen Van Tuong, Shanmugam Murugesu and Nelson Malachy, among many others, were waiting for the hangman to call.

In the top echelons of the drug trafficking world, the syndicate bosses are rarely caught and punished. They are able to live in the security of their fortified mansions, protected not only by armed bodyguards but by paying huge bribes—or doing deals—with their pursuers. Guiga Lyes Ben Laroussi is a typical case. Even after his arrest on a capital charge of trafficking, he managed to 'negotiate' with the Singapore authorities and have the charges drastically reduced so that his life would be spared in exchange for a twenty to thirty year prison term topped with twenty lashes of the rattan. And Guiga, the handsome thirty-five-year-old Tunisian holding down a high-paying executive position in Singapore, was allowed bail with a personal bond of S$280,000 in cash—paid, no doubt, with the proceeds of his nefarious activities. Although it was said he was ordered to surrender his passport as part of the arrangement he still managed to flee the country a few days later. How he did it so easily is no longer a mystery. In strict confidence a trusted informant revealed: 'As soon as he got bail, his passport was returned and he was told to leave immediately. It was arranged at a very high level.' Guiga and his powerful associates in his drug ring had obviously planned his getaway the moment Singapore's Central Narcotics Bureau officers swooped on his luxury home in Seletar in October 2004 and charged him.

'Guiga was very lucky to get bail,' said his lawyer, Subhas Anandan. 'But it was a bailable offence in his case,' he insisted. 'He called me from Tunisia not long ago—that's where he said he was—and asked me if I could help his girlfriend [Mariana Abdullah]. I told him, "No, I don't think I can." She's back in jail now for consumption,' added Anandan in his candid way. 'She has a very serious drug problem. Guiga is quite safe where he is. If a decision is made to extradite him, it will never succeed. Singapore will never be able to bring him back here. He's quite powerful in his own country, his family is well connected and the Tunisian police won't touch him. If they attempt to arrest and extradite him on behalf of Singapore, he and his family will tell them to go fly a kite! He probably travels on a false passport anyway, or has changed his name. Perhaps he's even changed his features by surgery!'

But, of course, with his influential, high-level connections in Singapore that would never be necessary, anyway. Guiga, as marketing manager at Bobby Rubino's, was in a perfect position to meet the 'right' people—socialites with little to occupy their minds and with too much cash in their wallets and purses, one of his close friends told me. Although he was already highly paid they provided him with a lucrative source of additional income, giving him millionaire status. Narcotics officers had been tailing him for two months and had spotted him on several occasions meeting suspected drug addicts outside nightclubs and bars in various parts of Singapore. Nevertheless, when the drugs found in his possession were weighed a second time they were suddenly well below the mandatory hanging offence. There was no mention of the dossier the CNB had compiled over the months of their surveillance. This, of course, is exactly what happened in the case of Julia Bohl, to prevent her large and powerful country, Germany, coming to economic blows with the diminutive Singapore. But in this case the astute Guiga and his high society pals had their own game plan. During the CNB investigation he refused to name any of his other customers—while hinting there were more prominent members of Singapore's high society he could expose as serious drug users which would create an even bigger scandal among the country's elite. His secret list of clients was his bargaining chip when the time was right, when the shadow of the gallows loomed. 'They were terrified that if he were to be tried for a capital offence with the gallows as the end game, he would first blow the lid off Singapore,' another lawyer close to the case told me.

After he managed a disappearing act even Harry Houdini might have envied, the authorities issued a statement to the media saying that if he were ever arrested and brought back to Singapore and tried he could still face the death penalty. There were also suggestions that Marx Oh Chee Wee could still be charged with the capital offence of trafficking if Guiga was brought back. But it is very unlikely that will ever happen. For obvious reasons, it seems that no one is really interested in pursuing the case further. Let sleeping dogs lie, seems to be the policy.

After the various trials and with the Tunisian drug baron safely in his home country, CNB deputy director S. Vajkumar issued a strong warning on his website: 'We do not go easy on our enforcement on drugs. We will spare no community that gets involved.' Laroussi must have smiled at this threat wherever he was at the time. He knew that the last time an expatriate was hanged in Singapore was in 1991 when Dutchman Johannes van Damme went to the gallows after being caught in transit at Changi Airport with 4.3 kilograms of heroin.

On 10 February 2010 Interpol updated its website, again featuring the fugitive on its list of wanted criminals for the fifth year running. It announced in its usual terse wording:

Guiga, Lyes Ben Laroussi, family name Guiga, date of birth June 14, 1969, place of birth: Le Bardo, Tunisia; languages spoken French and English. Height: 6′ 3″. Black hair. Offences: Drugs related crimes illegal possession and illegal traffic. Arrest warrant issued in Singapore. The appeal: IF YOU HAVE ANY INFORMATION CONTACT YOUR LOCAL OR NATIONAL POLICE.

I decided to respond to this appeal. Just before the publication of the first edition of this book, I called Singapore police and the CNB. 'I have it on good authority that Mr Laroussi is living with his family in Le Bardo, Tunisia,' I told them. I also put a call in to the current president of Interpol, former Singaporean police chief, Mr Khoo Boon Hui, to add weight to the urgency of the situation. People like Guiga Lyes Ben Laroussi are a menace to any society and should be hanged, I told him, parroting Senior Minister Goh Chok Tong when he explained why Nguyen Van Tuong had to be hanged a few months earlier. But despite the calibre of the men and women on his trail, this fugitive has now been on the run for almost six years.

In March 2010, Mr Khoo, in his capacity as president of Interpol, issued a red alert for the arrest of a runaway Romanian diplomat, Dr Silviu Ionescu, wanted for the hit and run death of a Singaporean. Ionescu had fled home amid screaming headlines in the *New Paper* and *Straits Times*, enraging Singaporeans who demanded the diplomat be arrested and brought back to face the consequences. If Mr Khoo could authorise a red alert for him, why not for Guiga, who might have been responsible for the deaths and destruction of many, many young lives? But Guiga's escape from the hangman did not even make the pages of the government-controlled *Straits Times*. Proof again that this scandal had to be covered up. Not surprising, either. As lawyer Subhas Anandan hinted to me, the reason Guiga was allowed to fade into obscurity is that no one wants this drug baron brought back to face the consequences for fear he might reveal even bigger names that would rock the island state to its foundations. That was his threat. And that's how *he* escaped the noose.

16

THE STING

Vignes Mourthi's journey to the gallows began on 20 September 2001. He was the son of an Indian-Malaysian couple who ran a small coffee shop near their home in Ipoh, Malaysia. Many immigrants from India, as well as first and second generation Indians in that part of Malaysia, worked in the large rubber and oil palm plantations. Vignes Mourthi's parents had both worked on a rubber plantation where they met when they were young and eventually managed to scrape together enough money to open the coffee shop. They did not make much from the business, barely enough to support themselves and their family of four children. Seeing far better job opportunities in Singapore—to many Malaysians the land of milk and honey just across the causeway from Johor Bahru—Vignes Mourthi, then eighteen, headed south.

Singapore is, of course, renowned for its bustling economy and its hard-working labour force. But many members of that labour force are not Singaporeans at all. In fact, the economy would take a rapid plunge if it suddenly had to make do without the thousands of lowly paid foreign workers contributing to its impressive GDP. Many of these foreign workers live in Johor where living costs are much lower and commute to work in Singapore where pay is much higher. This is what young Vignes Mourthi had decided to do. He found a low-rent house in a semi-derelict part of the border town, a job in Singapore, and commuted back and forth six days a week. By September 2001, he was working as a machine operator and packer for a freight company earning S$1400 per month, a handsome sum for someone of his background and education but rather modest by Singaporean standards.

Although by the time he was twenty-one Vignes Mourthi had married, he was able to send back two-thirds of his salary every month to his family in Ipoh. It was an arranged marriage and his wife, Pushpa, found a job in a local factory to help the domestic budget. Despite all these responsibilities and the daily motorcycle commute across the border in drenching rain or sweltering sunshine, his life appeared to be going well. Until 15 September 2001, that is, when he met with an accident on his motorcycle on his way home. The injury to his leg required expensive medical attention, he was unable to work for several days and his motorcycle was wrecked. It seems that an old family friend from Ipoh, Moorthy Angappan, heard about his accident and called by his home one evening for a chat. Angappan, a twenty-seven-year-old lorry driver, was more a friend of his father and when he moved with his family to a nearby town in Johor, he had promised to keep his eye on Vignes Mourthi. Angappan regarded him like a younger brother, it was said, but they had not seen each other since the youngster had moved south.

During the friendly chat, Angappan asked him if he would make a delivery to a friend in Singapore as soon as he was well enough to return to work. The 'delivery' turned out to be two plastic-wrapped packets, one white and one red. Angappan told him they contained incense stones used in Hindu ceremonies. As Vignes Mourthi knew that Angappan once owned a company dealing in this religious commodity he thought nothing more of the request and readily agreed to do him this favour. Angappan told him his friend Tahir would give him S$8000 in cash at the same time. Although this was a huge sum, Mourthi told one of his lawyers, M. Ravi, that he thought this was to do with a poultry business Angappan was planning to start up. Vignes Mourthi told Angappan he would return to work the next day, riding pillion on a friend's motorcycle. Angappan said he would return 'a little later' with the 'incense stones'. 'A little later' turned out to be 2 am. The banging on the door woke up Vignes Mourthi's wife. She roused her husband, who sleepily trundled to the front door, took possession of the packages, put them on a small coffee table in the hallway and went back to bed.

The checkpoint at Johor Bahru was fairly quiet when Vignes Mourthi and his friend, Jayacelan, who worked for the same company, rode through at 5.30 am headed for the factory in Changi on the other side of the island. Around 8 am Vignes Mourthi called Tahir at the number Angappan had written on a slip of paper. Tahir told him he would try to borrow a car and pick up the packets later that morning. However, the pain in Vignes Mourthi's injured leg was becoming unbearable again and he was given the rest of the day off. He called Angappan and asked him to make the delivery himself because he needed to get back home and seek medical help. But Angappan urged him to stay put until Tahir turned up, saying that he would pick him up and bring him back to Johor later in the day. Mourthi called Tahir and told him of the change of plan. He would go to the An Nur Mosque at Woodlands and hand over the package there.

This time Mourthi borrowed Jayacelan's motorcycle for the journey. When he arrived he called Tahir's number again. The phone was answered by a man who called himself 'Segar' and told him Tahir had been called away and that he would take the packages instead. He was told to look out for a silver car with the licence plate 9073 that would arrive within twenty minutes. A short time later a silver car pulled up and a long-haired Indian man stepped out. Introductions complete, Mourthi then pulled the red plastic packet from his riding helmet, but before handing it over asked Segar about the money he was supposed to receive from Tahir. Segar pulled out a thick wad of notes and handed this to Mourthi who checked just briefly that it was the S$8000 he was supposed to pick up. Segar smiled and gave a thumbs-up. The young man thought this was a friendly sign of approval. In fact, it was a pre-arranged signal to eight of his associates, all officers of the Central Narcotics Bureau. They rushed from their hiding places and surrounded Vignes Mourthi. It was a very neat sting operation. Segar then introduced himself as Sergeant S. Rajkumar, an undercover officer. Vignes Mourthi's life was as good as over.

The above is based on Vignes Mourthi's account of what happened to him that day. Sergeant Rajkumar had another account. Moorthy Angappan, the family friend on his way from Johor to pick up Vignes Mourthi near the An Nur Mosque, had another version. His lawyer would later tell the High Court in Singapore that he was waiting near a fruit shop a short distance from the mosque when Mourthi called to ask if he had arrived. A short while later two cars drove up to a spot not far from where Angappan was waiting. Unknown to him at that stage, Mourthi was in one of the cars. He peered out of the window, identified the man wearing a grey shirt as Angappan and his 'brother'—a term of affection, not of blood relation. The head of the sting operation, ASP Krishnan, and another officer approached Angappan. They identified themselves as CNB agents and asked Angappan what he was doing lingering near the fruit shop. He said he was waiting for a friend but refused to name him. The officers then arrested him for being part of the drug transaction they had just intercepted. Angappan's life now had an expiry date as well. They were both taken in separate cars to Clementi Police Station to be interrogated.

Were they accomplices, dupes or false accusers? It was a tangled web with many loose ends that the CNB easily managed to unravel— they knew the entire story even before it began unfolding. But they had to prove their case in court. The lives of two young men were at stake. Vignes Mourthi insisted he was an innocent dupe who believed he was delivering 'incense stones', not heroin. He was just doing

Angappan, an old family friend, a favour. 'Moorthy [Angappan] told me it was incense stones,' he told his interrogators. 'I have never seen heroin before. I only knew it was some sort of drugs after I was arrested.' He did not question the large amount of money he was supposed to pick up because it would have been 'disrespectful' to question Angappan, an older person. It would be like asking Angappan intimate questions about his relations with his wife. He made several statements implicating Angappan, who, he said, had lied about the true nature of the transaction and tricked him into becoming a 'mule'. Any bond between them was now totally in shreds, and it was Angappan who had done the shredding, according to Vignes Mourthi. It did not help that his wife of only five months, totally shocked by what happened, left him. They never saw each other again. She refused to visit him in jail and made only a sworn statement confirming Angappan's visits to their home. The only other witnesses to back up Mourthi's story in court were his two sisters.

Angappan, likewise, denied everything. He claimed he was the hapless victim of a family friend, completely ignorant of the crime and set up by Mourthi, a man whom he had only sought to help out that day, thus putting himself in mortal danger. He denied even being at Mourthi's home on the evening of 19 September. In fact, he claimed he was attending a belated birthday party for a nephew many kilometres away in another town. He was home by 11 pm, watched television and then went to bed. He called family witnesses to confirm his claims. The only contact he had with Vignes Mourthi was around 10 am the day of his arrest, when he received two phone calls to bring him back to Johor. After the second call he agreed and his 'good turn' ended with him facing the death penalty as a drugs trafficker.

Sergeant Rajkumar, twenty-nine and an experienced officer, was not taking sides. In his eyes, both men were guilty, partners in a scheme to transport dangerous and illegal drugs into Singapore and sell them. And as so often happens in the world of drug dealers and drug agents, Rajkumar had a string of informers who provided him with tips in exchange for favours and considerations. One of these was the now mysterious Tahir, who had contacted the officer in early September and provided him with some juicy information. A Malaysian drug syndicate, mainly from the Indian community, had a sizeable amount of heroin to move. They were looking to sell it in booming Singapore where it attracted much higher prices than in Malaysia. Rajkumar quickly sprang into action. He told Tahir to try to set up a deal with this syndicate and he would pose as a potential buyer. He provided the informer with a mobile phone number so that the Malaysian dealers could contact him directly if they wished. In Rajkumar's account of events presented at the trials of Mourthi and Angappan, the first call came only at 11 am on Thursday 20 September. The syndicate had a pound of heroin and were ready to deal. The officer said he was very interested and immediately set up the sting operation with a nine-man team.

According to court records, Rajkumar said that when he was completing the transaction with Mourthi using the name 'Segar', he 'brusquely' asked him where the money was. He said he was in the car with his partner when he then demanded: 'Where's the stuff?' Mourthi replied that it was hidden somewhere near the mosque. He told him to get the money then follow him. He also asked the officer if he could trust the Chinese man in the car. 'Segar' told him not to worry, the man was his 'financier' and that 'without him, I cannot deal'. The officer had one more ploy after the exchange took place to have Vignes Mourthi firmly in the trap. When he asked if the 'stuff' was good, Vignes Mourthi proudly replied, 'It's very good. Watch and see. You are sure to come back to deal with me again.' At that point, Rajkumar gave the thumbs-up signal.

It was a case that was riddled with controversy. Vignes Mourthi, only twenty-one, denied to the bitter end that he knew he was carrying heroin and insisted that Angappan told him the packets contained incense stones. He had been duped. Angappan insisted Mourthi had betrayed him to save himself. The two were tried together in the High

Court and the case, which spread over a five-month period, ended in August 2002. They were seated side by side in the defendant's dock throughout and the hatred that developed between the two former friends was obvious to everyone in the court room. One observer wrote: 'At times, it almost seemed as if the state could save itself the costs of both trial and executions by simply leaving the two alone in a darkened room for ten minutes, allowing them the opportunity to strangle each other to death.' They were represented by different counsel—Vignes Mourthi by Phillip Lum and Moorthy Angappan by Lee Teck Leng. Evidence given by Angappan's relatives that he was with them at a birthday party the evening Mourthi claimed he visited him and later dropped off the packets was rejected by the trial judge, Tay Yong Kwang. In the end Mourthi was found guilty of trafficking not less than 27.65 grams of heroin while Angappan was found guilty of abetting the offence and both were sentenced to death. Mourthi's conviction seemed to have been based largely on a handwritten record of an incriminating conversation that allegedly took place between him and Rajkumar, when he was asked if the 'stuff' was good.

The appeal against Tay's verdict began on 25 November 2005. It was heard by a three-judge quorum: Chief Justice Yong Pung How, Judge of Appeal Chao Hick Tin and Justice Judith Prakash. Angappan was once again represented by Lee Tech Leng, assisted by Michael Soo Chia. Mourthi had new counsel, Subhas Anandan, one of the most high-profile criminal defence lawyers in Singapore. According to court records, Anandan argued that the trial judge erred in not giving this 'naïve young man' the benefit of the doubt. Mourthi was just another innocent dupe taken advantage of by a more sophisticated adult. In particular he challenged the hand-written record of Rajkumar's conversation with Mourthi. It was Anandan's contention that the reliability of this crucial information may have been open to question. He raised the possibility that it was recorded much later, perhaps more than two months after the sting.

The record of the conversation was not signed or dated and Anandan maintained that considering Mourthi's life hung in the balance, these facts presented a reasonable doubt as to his guilt.

On 22 January 2003 the Court of Appeal rejected both Mourthi's and Angappan's appeals, spurning all pleas to entertain reasonable doubt in favour of supporting the trial judge's decision. They were on their way to the gallows. Their only hope now was presidential clemency, a rare event in Singapore's legal history.

Human rights activist and lawyer M. Ravi entered the fray at this stage on behalf of Mourthi. He had been approached by the condemned man's desperate family, who were struggling financially after huge amounts in legal fees. Although Mourthi's father offered him S$3000, Ravi refused and agreed to do what he could pro bono. He studied the case, recruited the help of a renowned lawyer, the late J.B. Jeyaretnam, and embarked on three special motions requesting a retrial on the grounds that there had been a miscarriage of justice. This again centred on the conversation which Rajkumar put in evidence that showed Mourthi knew he was handling drugs and not incense stones as he claimed, and which the accused maintained never took place. The note produced in evidence recording the conversation bore no date and could have been written up at any time.

Neither Mourthi nor the defence lawyers at the original trial were aware that such a document existed before it was produced in court. Ravi said the trial judge relied heavily on it to convict his client. He also questioned the fact that the mysterious informant, Tahir, was never produced as a witness and had apparently vanished. On 25 September 2003, the then Chief Justice Yong Pung How, who had already been party to denying Mourthi's appeal, ruled that the case could not be reopened, as it had already gone through the courts.

At the end of this hearing the accused rose and addressed the bench. He said that he was not afraid to die, but if he was going to die the next morning, he wanted to know the reasons for his execution. The Chief Justice said the decision would be published in due course and everyone could find the reasons there. It was the third time in three weeks that Ravi had appeared in court to stop Mourthi from being executed, only to be told he had no case. The Chief Justice told him brusquely: 'As far as the law is concerned he has been found guilty and convicted. Not much point for you to go on.'

Ravi believes still that it was unfair for Yong and Chao to be called upon to issue a judgment against their own original decision. But he wanted his client to be acquitted, or at least retried, and spent almost three hours trying to persuade Yong, Chao and Tan. Thanking him at the end, the Chief Justice said: 'It has crystallised our thinking ... that you have no case.'

The Chief Justice ended the proceedings with the words: 'You can say he is innocent but as far as the law is concerned, he has been found guilty and convicted. You had better say goodbye to him, that's all you can do.' Mourthi was expected to hang the next morning. Ravi quickly drafted another appeal to the President, which he sent via email at 9 pm that same day. In this letter, a longish plea to the President in his capacity as 'guardian of the Constitution of the Republic of Singapore', he implored him to reconsider the unusual situation and at least issue a stay of execution. That final attempt to save Mourthi's life fell on deaf ears and Mourthi was hanged, along with Angappan.

In mid October 2003, just three weeks after the executions, the Court of Appeal released its reason for having denied that final appeal a matter of hours before the execution. Once a criminal appeal has been dealt with, explained Ravi, neither the Court of Appeal nor the High Court can re-open the case. Chief Justice Yong cited three precedents in rendering this decision. In one of these cases, *Lim Choon Chye v Public Prosecutor*, the appeal was dismissed even though the applicant asserted that fresh evidence proving innocence had turned up since the earlier denial of an appeal. In this case, the former Judge of Appeal, M. Karthiegesu, had stated that it was not the Singapore parliament's intention to allow appellants an 'indefinitely extended right of appeal'. Therefore, a second appeal could not be allowed in any case where an appeal had already been heard and dismissed—even if that case involved the death penalty and an irreversible error may have been made. Said Ravi: 'The October 13 2003 decision of the court was fairly short and sweet, written in clear and compelling language. I can only hope that on the day of its release, Vignes Mourthi, wherever he was, could finally appreciate the reasons why he was hanged, especially when he had personally made that request to see the written judgment.'

It was only by chance during my investigations that I discovered from unpublished legal documents the details of events that went on in secret after Vignes Mourthi's arrest, trial and execution. In any other country with a free press, what had been happening secretly behind the scenes almost from the moment Mourthi was arrested would have created uproar when it was revealed. But in Singapore—ranked 133rd in the Press Freedom Index 2009 by Paris-based Reporters without Borders—this scandal did not even make the headlines it deserved in the pages of the government-controlled *Straits Times*, the *New Paper* or *Today*. Had this shameful information been exposed, a precious life might well have been saved.

Sergeant S. Rajkumar, a senior officer with the Central Narcotics Bureau, was the prosecution's most valuable witness in Vignes Mourthi's trial. What was never revealed at any time until after Mourthi was hanged was the fact that while Rajkumar was helping to send this young man to the gallows, he was being investigated by officers of the Criminal Investigation Department (CID). It was Rajkumar's sworn testimony that sealed Mourthi's fate—but no one on the defence team had any notion at this time that Rajkumar himself was under investigation for the alleged rape and sodomy of a young woman the day after he arrested Vignes Mourthi, and for subsequent attempts to bribe her to drop the charges.

It wasn't until after Mourthi's execution and the eventual trial and jailing of Rajkumar and another police officer that I came across the full damning evidence of this CNB officer's own criminal activities.

Vignes Mourthi was arrested for drug trafficking on 20 September 2001. Rajkumar was arrested on 23 September—just two days after he arrested Vignes Mourthi—avowed his innocence and was released on bail. At the same time intense efforts were being made by Rajkumar's many friends in the CNB and a police friend at Clementi Police Station to persuade 'J' to withdraw her statement. The bribes involved large sums of money, which she refused. Balbir Singh, the only other officer convicted of corruption, told 'J' that Rajkumar was afraid his wife would have a miscarriage, his mother would commit suicide and his father have a heart attack. He also told her to think carefully before proceeding with the case. It would be embarrassing for her and her family as her name and picture would be published in the newspapers. None of this, of course, was true. His family was physically and mentally well and it would be illegal for the name and photo of a rape victim to be published in any newspaper.

There were frantic, secret meetings between Rajkumar, his police officer friends and his accuser in shopping malls and fast-food outlets during which he, his family and friends continued to offer large sums of money in exchange for withdrawing her allegations. All this intrigue was going on while Rajkumar was busy getting enough evidence together to ensure Mourthi would be found guilty and hanged.

Although the case against Rajkumar eventually went ahead, it was put on the backburner while the trial of Mourthi continued to its grisly end on the gallows. Rajkumar's trial began the following year, in 2004. A string of witnesses on both sides took the stand. Both Rajkumar and one of his friends, police officer Balbir Singh, were found guilty of corruption. District Court Judge Sia Aik Kor sentenced Rajkumar to fifteen months in prison and Singh to six months.

Ironically, Balbir Singh, a police officer for seven years, complained of the methods used during his interrogation by the officers of the CID. He claimed his first signed statement was only inked after he had been forced to go almost two days without sleep, that he had been interrogated in an exceedingly cold room and that they slipped in an extra statement page, which he signed without reading. These claims echoed the defence presented by Mourthi's trial lawyers, that he signed certain incriminating statements when he was worn out after gruelling interrogations and was unable to pay full attention to every single point he was admitting to.

But what is even more extraordinary is that the trial of Mourthi was not delayed until *after* the case against Rajkumar was thoroughly investigated and his trial completed. If he were found guilty of corruption, the courts would have known exactly what kind of man Rajkumar really was and questioned the reliability of the evidence. It would have justifiably given Mourthi the benefit of the doubt that he—not his accuser—was telling the truth. And if this officer's evil wasn't known at the highest level, it should have been. The Public Prosecutor, Bala Reddy, who led the prosecution team against Mourthi should have been made aware of the investigation involving Rajkumar's alleged criminality, and should therefore have demanded a postponement of Mourthi's trial. It would have been prudent—as well as just—for the case against Rajkumar to have been resolved first.

As was always said by anti-death penalty campaigners in Britain and other abolitionist nations, it is better for a guilty man to go free than an innocent man to be hanged. Had they had proof that Rajkumar was guilty of corruption in another case, his evidence against Mourthi could have been more wisely considered by his trial judges. But it was not until Mourthi was hanged that Rajkumar's trial began. When Rajkumar was sentenced, Judge Sia Aik Kor described his actions as 'so obviously corrupt by the ordinary and objective standard that he must know his conduct is corrupt'. The judge also cited a precedent which found his actions to be 'akin to an attempt to subvert the course of justice'.

In the event, District Court Judge Sia Aik Kor sentenced Rajkumar to fifteen months in prison and Singh to six months. Following Rajkumar's conviction, it might also have been prudent to thoroughly investigate his record in other cases he had been involved in which resulted in other drug traffickers ending up on the gallows. But by 22 January 2003 the Court of Appeal had already rejected Mourthi's appeal, spurning all pleas to entertain reasonable doubt in favour of supporting the trial judge's decision. He would be hanged together with his alleged accomplice, Angappan, at the convenience of the justice system.

I can reveal, after speaking in confidence to several lawyers on condition that I would not expose them to the authorities in any way, that more than just a few people in high places must have known about Rajkumar. So were they intent on keeping his corrupt deeds under wraps until Vignes Mourthi was hanged? 'They were all terrified that it might be revealed at a very inopportune time,' one lawyer told me. 'It would have thrown a very interesting spotlight on our justice system.'

Subhas Anandan himself told me, on the record: 'If the cop had been tried first Vignes' trial lawyers would have gone to town with it … I think Vignes would have got off because of the evidence of someone already convicted of corruption. The judge would have to think twice or three times before imposing a death sentence.'

17

HERO HANGED

Shanmugam Murugesu's hanging in May 2005 sparked unprecedented public discussion in Singapore. From April to August that year, local activists organised petitions, vigils and other events to campaign against the death penalty. But it wasn't easy. The authorities, using undercover police, did everything they could to thwart this bid to save the young man's life. Amnesty International sent a special representative to address a public forum. A worried government prevented him from speaking and banned the use of the condemned man's face on posters on the grounds that it would 'glorify' an executed convict. Shanmugam was convicted of trafficking 1.03 kilograms of cannabis. A former jet ski champion and army regular, he was a struggling divorced father of twin teenage sons. His sons pleaded for him in leaflets they distributed in a first-ever public appeal in a capital crime case. His mother made a tearful plea for him at the forum, which stunned forum participants. She also made an appeal that was captured on video.

Before he was sentenced to death, Shanmugam pleaded for clemency saying he 'was in desperate financial circumstances, which led me to commit the offence which I wholeheartedly regret. The financial burdens on me were heavy as I had to look after my sons, my nieces, nephews and my mother who is in poor health and unable to work.' His statement of regret proved futile. Enter again M. Ravi, who was still recovering emotionally, physically and financially following the Vignes Mourthi case. He did not charge the Mourthi family a cent for his legal services and, because they had become so impoverished after paying the trial and appeal lawyers, he paid $7000 for Vignes' funeral out of his own pocket. His efforts in the court room did not make him at all popular with the Singapore government. He had brought much foreign media attention while valiantly fighting to save the life of Vignes Mourthi. As a result, Ravi also saw some of his long-time, very well paying clients drop him as their solicitor because they feared that he was now viewed as an 'anti-establishment figure', association with whom would reflect negatively on them.

In fact, the Vignes Mourthi case was the first of its kind for Ravi. He normally dealt in areas of the law which paid well—civil litigation and intellectual property matters. And it made him reflect on what had really been accomplished. 'I hoped to get the people of Singapore thinking about the critical issues in the case,' he said, 'to widen public awareness of how the judicial system here worked and also to get large numbers of Singaporeans asking if this was indeed a system that needs no reforms or refinements. The whole question of executions was of major importance to me as was the question of who gets executed here and why.' Shanmugam Murugesu had read of the Mourthi case and he wanted to speak to Ravi.

Shanmugam, a Singaporean, was in custody facing the death penalty, having been arrested on 30 August 2003, just four weeks before Mourthi was executed. Shanmugam had been arrested at the Tuas Checkpoint, known as the second link joining Singapore to Malaysia, with six packets of cannabis weighing 1029 grams and 880 grams of cannabis mixture, over double the legal limit for mere possession in Singapore. He admitted he was a small-time dealer but vehemently denied that he was transporting anywhere near the amount they found tucked away on his motorcycle. According to court records of his statements he maintained that he had brought only one packet of cannabis into Singapore weighing only 237 grams. He was not a stupid man and was aware of the consequences of being found in possession of more than that amount. He revealed his Malaysian supplier as a man named Mok who often encouraged him to traffic more despite his constant refusals. He believed that the other five packets had been hidden in his bike by Mok, without his knowledge. To support his claim he even gave police Mok's name and telephone number, hoping they would investigate him. He gave police other kinds of information but they seemingly did not believe his story, especially that he had always dealt in small amounts of cannabis and that Mok always tried to get him to take on bigger assignments. Mok was apparently never found, let alone charged as an accomplice. This made me remember what I had been told by my anonymous informant who had once been an officer of the CNB. This man revealed to me that one of the practices of undercover agents was to encourage small-time dealers to traffic much more than they wanted to, thus ending up on the gallows. So was 'Mok' an undercover agent and if so did he deliberately act to send Shanmugam to the gallows?

It was while he was in a cell in Queenstown Remand Prison that Shanmugam heard about Ravi's valiant though futile fight to save Vignes Mourthi's life. Until his arrest, Shanmugam was something of a local hero. He had grown up in poverty, the eldest of a struggling Indian Singaporean family. Shanmugam was determined to make something of himself. But he was not a good scholar—he failed secondary school and began falling into bad company. His mother, Letchumi, a traditional conservative Tamil mother, took charge of his life and persuaded him to start over. He went back to school, his grades improved and eventually was accepted into Boys' School, something like the equivalent of a military academy. It was a fast track to the army, which is where Shanmugam ended up four years later. He had a solid record in his near ten years on active service, ended up with the rank of sergeant and seemed destined for the officers' ranks and a long career in the military. However, his marriage at the age of twenty-one served as a brake to his advancement in the army, when he found himself the father of twin sons. The demands on his time in the military were not good for a man with a young family.

After eight years in the army as a combat engineer, Shanmugam made an even more admired career move. He became a sports star. He had always shone in his athletic pursuits but what he loved most was water jet skiing. He was so skilled and daring that he even represented Singapore in the 1995 World Championship Jet Ski Finals in Lake Havasu, Arizona, USA, bringing home a medal, giving a huge and much-needed boost to Singapore's international image as a sports nation. He was also involved in motorbike racing, deep-sea diving, boating and rope climbing, all of them risky pursuits. As a result Shanmugam had many female admirers and friends but he never broke his wedding vows. His clean reputation also resulted in him being appointed to the prestigious Singapore Sports Council where he served for four years.

One of Shanmugam's sideline businesses was repairing all kinds of motorised land or sea vehicles, which kept him very busy. On the surface all seemed well but trouble was brewing in his marriage. It was an arranged union to a first cousin on his mother's side from India and it never became one of wedded bliss. After significant marital troubles, he divorced his wife and won custody of the twin boys, then twelve years old. His mother helped look after them.

Other things began to go wrong in his life and he lost interest in his sports activities. His mother fell ill and he found himself being the sole breadwinner for her and his unmarried sister. A promising new relationship with an attractive American woman also suddenly came to an abrupt end. She had second thoughts about becoming a mother to his sons and decided to return to the US. All this made him extremely depressed and he tried to escape in the haze of cannabis smoke. Shanmugam took jobs as a taxi driver and part-time window cleaner and sometimes repaired boats in Johor Bahru, the town where Vignes Mourthi had lived until his arrest. Occasionally Shanmugam would meet up privately with friends in Johor to smoke some weed, throwing in $20 each to purchase what they needed. One of them linked him up with Mok, who was to become the shadowy figure in his eventual demise. Mok had a motorbike and a boat with problems and Shanmugam was the man to fix them. He also joined Shanmugam in smoking weed with his other friends, which appeared to seal their friendship. Shanmugam had a reputation of being too trusting, even gullible. What happened next should have been a warning to him.

By this time Shanmugam was now supporting not only his own sons, his frail mother and single sister, but also a sister, Mahes, who had separated from her husband, and Mahes' two sons. The burdens on his shoulders, however broad and willing, were becoming too much for him. By a strange coincidence, his younger brother, Kuben, was a police officer and at one time was seconded to the Central Narcotics Bureau, but at this time he was a member of the marine police.

Except for a minor traffic offence, Shanmugam did not have a single previous conviction before that fatal day, 30 August 2003. He had decided, with Mok as his supplier, to help solve his financial problems by taking small amounts of cannabis into Singapore and selling it. He was always sure never to carry an amount weighing more than 500 grams and he only handled cannabis. He may have been too trusting of some people but he was not an idiot.

Unable to contact Ravi to take on his case, he was represented by two court-appointed counsel, Ganesan and Rajah Retnam. His trial was a total contrast to the action-packed trial of Vignes Mourthi and Moorthy Angappan, which dragged on for almost five months. Shanmugam's trial lasted exactly four days. The only witnesses called were the defendant himself, arresting and interrogating officers and police recorders—outnumbering him twenty-three to one—and a Tamil-language interpreter. 'The same evidence against him was repeated over and over like layers of cement preventing any mental daylight to creep in,' Ravi told me later after examining the case.

Shanmugam could only repeat that the other five packets totalling

1880 grams of cannabis and cannabis mixture had been secreted into cavities in his motorcycle by someone else, most likely the now mysterious Mok. He maintained that he knowingly had just under 300 grams in his possession—not a hanging offence. One point against Shanmugam was that he was slow in naming Mok as his supplier. His answer was that he did not want to get this man, whom he regarded as a friend, into trouble. But as time went on, especially after revealing all he knew about him, he was certain Mok was the one who landed him in all this trouble.

The trial began on 19 April 2004. Judge Tay Yong Kwang decided that Shanmugam's account was 'highly unlikely to be true'. Shanmugan also claimed he had been 'severely intimidated' during his interrogation, with officers shouting at him, even slapping him on the side of his head several times. In Singapore suspects have no right to legal counsel during interrogations and very rarely do any lawyers even get to see their clients during the early stages of their confinement. The prosecution denied all these allegations, however, and persuaded the court that it was Shanmugam's intention to smuggle a larger amount of cannabis purely to make a larger amount of money. At 11.46 am on 23 April Judge Tay adjourned to his chambers to consider his verdict. He must have already made up his mind. He was back at 11.59 am. The verdict was guilty. The sentence was death.

Shanmugam arrived on death row that evening. Darshan Singh would soon be busy weighing and measuring this fit young man, and noting his muscularity. But first the routine appeals stage had to be gone through. Shanmugam's second lawyer was Peter Fernando, who had handled many drug cases over a long career with an enviable record of successful defences—but not necessarily capital offences. His appeal, filed on 25 October 2004, was again heard before Chief Justice Yong Pung How with Judge Chao Hick Tin and Kan Ting Chiu. It was just routine, with both sides repeating what had already been said at the original trial. The appeal was, predictably, dismissed. All Shanmugam could do now was to sit on death row and pray for presidential clemency. The chances were grim. Only six had been granted in the forty-year history of the Republic. A miracle would be more likely. But if the government was angry with attorney and human rights activist M. Ravi for exposing Singapore's justice system in the Vignes Mourthi case, they were in for a bigger surprise this time.

The zealous lawyer took up the cause before the President's clemency ruling was issued, realising that the odds were against getting a clemency ruling. This time he took a different tack, a new strategy. He decided to take the battle to the court of public opinion as well. His ideas soon won the approval of Shanmugam's family, including his police officer brother, Kuben.

In the petition to the President which his appeal lawyers had prepared, the team cited six cases from just the previous two years in which individuals had been arrested for possession of cannabis wherein the amount was officially reduced to 499 grams, allowing the defendant to escape the death penalty. In five of the cases the original amounts of cannabis had been higher than what Shanmugam himself was caught with. The petition also included letters attesting to his character from his two sons, both his parents, his former girlfriend now living back in America and his brother, Kuben, the Singapore policeman. The case for clemency looked good, but Ravi felt it needed something more. And there wasn't much time before the President made his decision.

He launched a public relations campaign, printing up hundreds of flyers on the case and distributing them. These flyers were handed out primarily at Centrepoint, a popular shopping and dining complex along Singapore's Orchard Road. While Shanmugam's sons played the major role in distribution, other volunteers also came forward to help out. Unusually, the local press took notice of this action and gave the story some valuable space. Photos of the twins offering flyers to passersby made for good attention grabbers. The photos attracted the attention and support of many, including some opposition political figures, such as Dr Chee Soon Juan, the head of Singapore's Democratic Party and a long time campaigner for civil rights. Chee and Ravi then organised a special forum on the death penalty itself, printing more flyers and booking a meeting hall at the Asia Hotel. They had expected about seventy to turn up but they totalled almost 200. This number included me along with several plainclothes police officers from the much-feared Internal Security Department. Talks on the death penalty were given by the condemned man's lawyers and Dr Chee. The emotional high point was a plea by Letchumi Ammah for her son's life. This brief appeal, delivered in Tamil, then translated into English by Ravi, stirred almost everyone in the room and brought tears to the eyes of many.

Tim Parritt from Amnesty International had been invited to speak at the forum. He flew in from Kuala Lumpur specifically for the event. However, the day before he was informed by the Singapore government that he would not be permitted to speak. He was free to come in but if he opened his mouth he would most likely be arrested. Parritt naturally wished to show his solidarity with the cause, so he took his assigned place of honour, then sat silently on the stage with the other scheduled speakers while his prepared speech was read out by the event's moderator, Saliah Ahmad. She was then approached by two plainclothes officers who questioned her and demanded to see her passport proving she was a Singapore citizen. There was nothing more they could do but their action put a damper on the event and the forum was shortly brought to a close.

But its impact created quite a stir locally and internationally. People from the local arts community put together a three-hour vigil with music, poetry, dance and theatre to energise everyone on this issue. Reporters and photographers from the Associated Press, Agence France-Presse and Reuters turned up in full force. Even the *Straits Times* relaxed its straitjacket buttons just a tad and sent a reporter to record the goings on.

Later a dedicated group of thirty headed off to the Istana, the President's palace, to make yet another personal appeal to the President to grant clemency. They were bent on making this appeal as effective as possible. In at least one regard, it produced an undeniable effect. Observers noted that there were probably more police than petitioners there, many of them Internal Security Department officers. So that they would not get arrested for 'unlawful assembly' the demonstrators split into groups of four—otherwise they could have been carted off in black Marias to spend the night in a detention centre on a cold concrete block of a bed with only a smelly, bug-infested blanket to keep them warm, then hauled before a court the next morning and fined.

The most dramatic moment in the impromptu demonstration came when Shanmugam's mother and sons knelt down before the Istana's gates and implored the president to grant the convicted man a reprieve. A Reuters photographer had gone with the group to shoot photos of the protests. Over the next few days dramatic images of Letchumi and the boys were flashed around the world. The impact was stunning. Never before in the history of the city-state had an impending presidential clemency ruling drawn such widespread attention.

Less than a week later, President Nathan issued his ruling. Despite all the activities of the previous few weeks, the appeal was rejected. Was this just a demonstration to the world that Singapore's rulers would not be moved by such protests? Just consider the difference in the treatment Julia Bohl received when the German government stepped in and saved her life. Had Shanmugam's name been Schönfeld and had he been born in Dortmund, the outcome would have been entirely different. He had no valuable currency, no huge trade deal to offer.

Ravi, a man I am proud to know, felt sick when he read the President's decision, which was sent straight to his office. He shook his head. 'I really couldn't understand this president, denying clemency to a man who seemed to be a perfect candidate for such a show of mercy,' he told me later. Ravi asked himself what had gone through the Head of State's mind as he weighed all the factors in coming to this decision. He then had the awful duty of telling Shanmugam's family. When he arrived at their home, a housing development flat in Jurong West district, only his mother, Letchumi, and her elderly aunt were at home.

What happened next is something he will never erase from his memory. 'For a few minutes,' he said, 'she just stood there, numb with shock.' Then, he recalled, she started beating her own face with her fists, then dropped her hands and started drumming hard on her chest. Finally, she screamed and almost collapsed on the floor in grief. Well aware of her poor physical health, Ravi was afraid she was about to have a stroke, or was maybe already in the throes of one. The tension and pain in her body, he said, seemed to have taken on an intensity of their own.

Ravi had never been the recipient of such a notification from the President before and said he was 'surprised' at the rather cold handling of this matter. The letter was sent by regular mail and took four days to reach his office. 'I thought that the Head of State, generally known for his courtesy and congeniality, could have accorded this one small courtesy to the family of a condemned man.' Just as bizarrely, Ravi revealed, Shanmugam received a medal for his achievements as an army reservist, which was presented to him around the time of the clemency decision. Obviously, the clemency committee had not allowed this honour, or any of the previous honours, to influence them in their deliberations.

Ravi and his supporters lined up one more major event before the scheduled execution. It was a vigil planned by Lee Weng Choy of the Substation Arts Complex and Lucy Davis, along with Sinapan Samydorai, head of the Think Centre. The Substation offered a garden performance area at the rear of the complex that would have been ideal for such an event. The various acts could perform in the open air on a large open stage. Moreover, a candlelight vigil for the condemned man could be held there with no fear of violating fire laws or endangering participants. The police got wind of their plans, however, and banned the event on the grounds that it was in an open space and things could get out of control.

The group then approached the Golden Landmark Hotel on Beach Road and booked a reception room appropriate for their needs. Sinapan was the official organiser. Just three days before the event, he received a call from the hotel with some bad news. There was a leak in the roof and they had to cancel the booking. 'It was more likely a leak to the police,' said Ravi. 'We speculated that pressure had been put on the hotel to prevent the vigil.' Ravi then booked a room at the Furama Hotel near Chinatown and the vigil went ahead more or less as planned. It was held in the Canton Meeting Room and lasted more than three hours. There were bands, solo musicians, a cappella singers and poetry readings. Ravi got up to talk about Shanmugam's demise and the death penalty. Others followed him.

But not everyone wanted to speak, read, play or sing in protest at the pending execution. Members of Singapore's police department in plainclothes happened to drop by. And when people not listed to speak were invited to, the police stepped forward and stopped them, threatening arrest if they continued to defy the law. One of these was V.A. Sivakumar of the Vallalar organisation, a Hindu group opposed to all killing for any reason. He was stopped from talking immediately, his name and address taken down by two police officers. Shanmugam's mother and his sons were also present and all this only added to their misery.

An article about the vigil appeared in the *Guardian*, one of Britain's most respected newspapers, the next day. Headed 'Singapore Finally Finds A Voice In Death Row Protest', the article proclaimed that history had been made at the Furama Hotel where 'an unprecedented event for the tightly controlled island republic' had been held. John Aglionby, a veteran journalist with the UK

Guardian and *Sunday Observer* was sent from Jakarta to cover this ground-breaking event. The headline above Aglionby's article, which appeared in that *Sunday Observer*, began: 'A Silence Broken.' And there was indeed, said Ravi, an invigorating sense of silence being broken. Sadly, whatever this vigil did accomplish, it did not save Shanmugam from the noose. The execution date was immediately after the vigil: Friday, 13 May 2004.

18

PLEASE DON'T LET THEM KILL ME!

'Please don't let them kill me. I don't understand why they have to kill somebody for something like this.' This haunting cry from a terrified young man was ringing in lawyer M. Ravi's ears as he walked through the gates of Changi Prison into the sunlight. He had just said his final farewell to his client Amara Tochi, who was due to hang at dawn the following day. It was a tearful moment for them both. Ravi had done all he could to prevent the killing of this likeable, handsome young man, a talented footballer who had come to Singapore to fulfil a dream. For the twenty-one-year-old kid from a dirt poor village in Nigeria, Ravi was his last hope. He knew he would be dead the next day.

Earlier that morning, the Court of Appeal refused to commute the death sentences on Tochi and his alleged accomplice Okele Nelson Malachy, a thirty-three-year-old South African, for trafficking 727.02 grams of heroin into the country. Ravi had worked ceaselessly to save Tochi, first in the Appeal Court then, as a last resort, with a desperate plea for clemency from President S.R. Nathan. Tochi said he thought he was carrying African herbs that tasted like chocolate, and even ate one capsule, according to the evidence, to show the police it was 'safe', a gesture suggesting either complete ignorance or naïveté.

The court delivered the death sentence after a thirteen-day trial during which even Judge Kan Ting Chiu himself raised reasonable doubts about the alleged crime before sentencing Tochi to death.

Tochi had left his poverty-stricken village in Nigeria three years earlier and headed for Dubai hoping to find a football club willing to give him a chance to achieve fame and fortune. He had just turned eighteen and had little education, having dropped out of school at fourteen. But his skill as a player was impressive. He was such a promising player he went to Senegal to join Njambi Football Club, where he so impressed his mentors he was picked to play for Nigeria in the quarter-final in the West African Coca-Cola Cup. Tochi then returned to his village to plan another career move. He wanted to widen his experience and become a world-class player—and above all help his family get out of its poverty cycle. A football coach told him there were opportunities in Dubai for talented, determined young African players like him. With only a few hundred dollars in his pocket he travelled by plane and train to Islamabad in Pakistan to obtain a visa for the Arab Emirates.

There his plans began to go awry. His visa application was refused. He did not have enough documentation and the little money he had was running out. He was stranded and alone in a strange country. 'I was in total despair,' he wrote in his diary in his cell on death row in Changi Prison on 4 August 2006, six months before he was hanged. 'No accommodation, no food and little money.' He went to Saint Andrew's Church in Islamabad for help. 'Pastor Andy was very kind to allow me to stay,' he wrote.

During a Sunday service at Saint Andrew's, Tochi met 'Mr Smith', another African from the same Igbo-speaking language group. He told Tochi he was an engineer and even recognised him as the player who missed a penalty that cost his team the match. 'It was a state league match in Nigeria in 2003,' wrote Tochi.

> I represented United FC. I felt shy about the missed penalty but later summoned enough courage and admitted to Mr Smith I was the one. He said they play only cricket in Pakistan, not football. Then I told him

my story. From time to time he used to give me money for my survival and buy me food. I met him again in a restaurant when he told me he could help me get a visa to enter Dubai. He said there was a Dubai Embassy in Afghanistan. He took my passport and we went there together by plane.

Tochi's visa application was again refused. He needed much more documentation from his homeland to prove who he was. Smith assured him all would be well. 'Not to worry,' Smith kept assuring the youngster. 'He said he would take care of me,' continued Tochi in his diary. It was clear that he did not fully realise whose hands he was now in. Tochi then described being flown back to Dubai to catch a connecting flight to Singapore where, Smith assured him, he would be able to apply for trials with the football federation. Smith would pay for the flight and his basic expenses. And, as a favour, would he take some special African herbs for his best friend, a 'Mr Marshall'? He was also African and sick with a serious stomach ailment and needed them desperately. In return 'Mr Marshall' would give him US$2000 to enable him to enter Singapore on a thirty-day visa— enough time and money to obtain a long-term work pass and achieve his football dream.

When Tochi arrived at Terminal 2's transit lounge there was no sign of Marshall. He should have been at the pre-arranged meeting point, an ubiquitous Coffee Bean and Tea Leaf café. After waiting six hours, he called Smith, who was by then back in Pakistan. He was worried he would be stranded again if Marshall did not turn up with the promised money in exchange for the herbs. Without it, he would be sent back to Dubai, a country that would not let him enter either. His future seemed very dire indeed. But he was assured that Marshall would turn up soon. Exhausted by the wait and travel, Tochi decided to check into the airport's Ambassador Hotel and get some rest. The receptionist noticed he did not have a visa and advised him that he would be sent back to Dubai the next day without one. Tochi explained he was waiting for his friend to arrive with enough money for him to enter Singapore. The receptionist told him she was duty bound to inform the airport police. Twenty minutes passed before the police turned up. While he was waiting for them, Tochi strolled around the transit lounge unconcerned by the fact that the police would want to know all about him and the 'African herbs' he had in his bag. The police came and questioned him. Then they looked in his bag. Tochi's football dreams had come to an abrupt end.

After his trial in the High Court ended on 22 December 2005, Tochi was found guilty and sentenced to death. Marshall's real name turned out to be Okele Nelson Malachy and his true nationality was never determined. He was described as a stateless African who had arrived in Singapore using a forged passport. He was also sentenced to death for trafficking the same 727.02 grams of diamorphine (or heroin) into Singapore even though he never took possession of the capsules.

Ravi, Tochi's second lawyer, fought a losing battle in a frantic bid to save him. He appealed against the sentence and asked for a retrial. This was denied. Then he made the desperate plea for clemency.

'It is disturbing to note,' Ravi told me after Tochi was hanged, 'that the learned trial judge himself raised reasonable doubts as to his guilt.' In paragraph 42 of his judgment, trial judge Kang Chiu said: 'There was no direct evidence that he knew the capsules contained diamorphine. There was nothing to suggest that Smith told him that the capsules contained diamorphine, or that he had found that out on his own—but he should have.' In paragraph 48, Judge Kang wrote: 'I found he had wilfully turned a blind eye on the contents of the capsules because he was tempted by the US$2000, which was a large sum to him. Consequently, even if he may not have actual knowledge that he was carrying diamorphine, his ignorance did not exculpate him.'

Against Malachy, he said: 'Although there was no direct evidence that the accused knew that the capsules contained drugs, there is no presumption of such knowledge raised against him.' He then proceeded to convict both men and sentenced them to death.

Ravi maintains that criminal laws of Singapore are unjust.

They are completely weighted against the accused. For example, confession alone can be relied upon in sentencing a person to death. Also there is no right to pre-trial discovery on accused statements or admissions. It is almost impossible to rebut the presumption where the burden is reversed on the accused to prove his innocence. Further, an accused person can be convicted solely on the uncorroborated and unsupported evidence of a co-accused. The courts here have moreover declared they have no jurisdiction or powers to reopen a case even if there is fresh evidence adduced before execution.

The night before Tochi and Malachy were hanged, I joined a candlelight vigil outside Changi Prison attended by barely a dozen Singaporeans, testament to the secrecy the government maintains. At the vigil, prominent Singapore-based art critic Lee Weng Choy said he disagreed with Singapore's mandatory death sentence, which he said takes away the discretionary power of the judiciary. 'I also disagree with its justification as a deterrent. The reality is that drug trafficking has not been reduced to zero, neither has drug use,' he said.

The execution of Tochi was carried out despite an appeal by Nigerian President Olesegun Obasanjo who asked Singapore Prime Minister Lee Hsien Loong to commute the death sentence. Lee maintained that Tochi had committed a serious offence under Singapore law and had exhausted all legal options. 'We did not take the decision lightly,' Lee wrote in a letter. 'I realise that Mr Tochi's family will find Singapore's position difficult to accept, but we have a duty to safeguard the interests of Singaporeans, and protect the many lives that would otherwise be ruined by the drug syndicates.'

Ravi believes African nationals in particular caught trafficking drugs in Asia get different treatment. He cited a spate of executions which had largely gone unnoticed, and some Westerners like Julia

Bohl and Michael McCrea who escaped the gallows. 'It's clear', he said, 'that Africans are treated in a discriminatory manner and their cases rarely get the attention of the international or local media. Many young African males are lured to Asia by attractive sports and athletic deals but end up being exploited as petty drug traffickers.'

Ravi said the mandatory death sentence in Singapore was declared unlawful by the United Nations in November 2005. He flew to Lagos to lend his assistance to Nigeria and South Africa to refer the matter to the International Court of Justice and to argue the case. He also lobbied the American Bar Association, Amnesty International and the Australian Coalition against the Death Penalty, and carried his campaign across Europe to highlight this grave situation. Ravi vows that he will spend the rest of his life, if necessary, fighting to abolish the mandatory death sentence in Singapore if not the death penalty in totality.

As with other protests, the campaigners outside Changi Prison were obliged to gather in groups of no more than four otherwise they would have been arrested for 'unlawful assembly'. Tochi's red football jersey, which was given to Ravi by Tochi as a farewell present, was hung on the prison fence with many candles lit around it. As the time of the hanging approached, many people who were gathered outside the prison sat down and quietly bowed their heads to say their silent goodbyes to the young Nigerian. 'There was no need to kill him,' said Ravi angrily. 'Even if he had some idea what he was doing was wrong, was it worth snuffing out such a promising young life?'

At dawn on Friday, 26 January 2007 these two African men who had never met before their arrests were hanged simultaneously in Changi Prison. The executions received scant attention in the local and world media. The news was announced in a brief statement by an assistant superintendent at Singapore's Central Narcotics Bureau. Tochi's family had not travelled to Singapore to see him because they could not afford the journey, according to an official at the Nigerian embassy. A lawyer representing the family flew to Singapore hoping to pass on personal messages of love from his parents and other family members but even he was denied permission to see Tochi before he was hanged.

I have written very little about Nelson Malachy, the man Tochi was destined to meet at a table in the Coffee Bean and Tea Leaf café and who had never heard of him until he arrived in Singapore from Dubai courtesy of Smith. While investigating all these characters I began wondering who 'Mr Smith' really was. Did he matter to the Central Narcotics Bureau who prosecuted Tochi and Malachy on behalf of the Singapore government? In fact, did Malachy matter to the judge who heard his trial and sentenced him to death? According to court records Malachy was a stateless person, sometimes described as a South African. But there was no one in the court to speak up for him. No diplomat from the High Commission, no one from his family. As far as everyone was concerned he did not have one. Malachy was defenceless in his anonymity. He was nobody. Just another black man. He did not exist. And he, too, was easy prey for Singapore's judicial system. More importantly, there was no campaigning newspaper in Singapore carefully following the trials of these men which might have sounded the alarm bells that yet another miscarriage of justice might be taking place.

19

A WOMAN OF NO IMPORTANCE

With Singapore's much-vaunted recovery program for drug addicts and Changi Prison's proud motto 'Captains of Lives: Rehab, Renew, Restart' one would have thought thirty-seven-year-old hairdresser Yen May Woen would have been in safe, caring hands. As a serious heroin addict, she would definitely have qualified for special treatment in a bid to return her to normality. Yen, a Singaporean, was a victim of a broken home. During her teen years, Yen dreamed of one day finding a good man to marry and raise a family with. Her special wish was to be given away by her father, wearing a beautiful white wedding dress. After her parents divorced her life spun out of control. She began using drugs such as marijuana to ease the pain and mixed with the wrong company. As the years passed she gravitated to heroin and ice. As so often happens, her circle of friends was targeted by the narcotics police after a tip-off and an undercover agent joined in, carefully taking note of what she and the others were doing. Unable to find regular employment she began trafficking the drug to fund her habit.

She was charged with trafficking in not less than 30.16 grams of diamorphine, or heroin, on 8 May 2002. A team of Central Narcotics Bureau officers was instructed to look for her near a taxi stand at Block 179 Toa Payoh Central. They saw her arrive in a taxi which stopped a short distance from the taxi stand. 'She alighted,' one of the officers recorded, 'and brought a black sling bag to the boot of the taxi and closed the boot. She then went to meet a male Chinese near the taxi stand while the taxi remained where it had stopped.'

The officers moved in and arrested Yen, the man and the driver of the taxi. It was obvious the officers knew what they were doing. The boot of the taxi was opened in her presence. Once of the officers, Senior Staff Sergeant Tan Yian Chye saw the sling bag and questioned her in Hokkien. The English translation of the exchange, according to court records, reads:

Q: This bag, does it belong to you?
A: Accused nods her head.
Q: What is inside the bag?
A: Inside the bag contained more than 30 packets of heroin.

Later, still at the scene of the bust, another officer, Station Inspector Ronnie See Su Khoon, arrived to take over the investigation. His recorded statement reads:

Q: This black colour bag belongs to whom?
A: It's mine.
Q: What is inside?
A: Heroin.
Q: What this heroin meant for?
A: Consume.
Q: Whom you obtain the heroin from?
Accused shook her head.
Q: Do you have anything else to say?
Accused shook her head.

Yen was taken to CNB headquarters at the Police Cantonment Complex and charged with trafficking 120 sachets of diamorphine. Inspector Neo Ling Sim recorded her one-line response: 'I did not know there was so much heroin.' Subsequently, according to court records, a series of five investigation statements were recorded from her between 10 May and 20 August 2002. These revealed that on the day of her arrest, a friend 'Tua Kang' telephoned her and arranged to return to her some cash and a cheque arising from a football bet; she called her drug supplier 'Jack' and ordered a week's supply of twenty to thirty sachets of heroin and some ice from him, and collected and paid for the drugs at Thomson Place. That was when the police pounced.

Yen said she was 'high' at the time of her arrest and in a state of fatigue. She also said she was very frightened and at a loss when she realised that there was so much heroin in the bag. She felt that she would not be believed if she said the heroin did not belong to her, and thought that if she admitted that twenty to thirty sachets belonged to her she would evade the death penalty. She also claimed that when she made those statements, 'I did not take heroin for a few days and I felt very lousy.'

There was no plea-bargaining for Yen while a deal was being worked out. She was found guilty as a matter of course. Judge Boo Bih Li said she had not rebutted the presumption under the *Misuse of Drugs Act* that she was in possession of the heroin for the purpose of trafficking. Very little was said in court about Yen's background and how she came to such a dire end.

The government-controlled media gave very little ink or airtime to the case, merely reporting the basic details. No mass media coverage for her, no powerful country or organisation using its muscle to try to prevent yet another judicial hanging—only a court-appointed lawyer. There were no anti-death penalty demonstrations outside the court when the verdict was announced. Yen didn't stand a chance even in her own country surrounded by millions of fellow citizens who would be too scared, gutless or disinterested to say boo to the system, even if they really knew what goes on under their noses. Hardly anyone knew about her case, let alone lifted a finger to help her. She was not a foreigner from a country prepared to use its economic muscle to protect her; she was not one of those they give impossibly long jail sentences to or thrash with the rattan; she did not come from the higher echelons of society and live in the nicest parts of the city.

It was unfortunate for Yen that she was born to a poor family in a less salubrious neighbourhood—a million miles from the likes of Sentosa, Goodwood Park and Balmoral Park. She needed the money only to fund her habit. She and two co-conspirators had been under surveillance. Undercover officers had been watching their every move, waiting for the right time to strike. Yen was quickly tried, sentenced to death and hanged soon afterwards with hardly anyone in Singapore knowing anything about her plight.

As ever, there were no campaigning journalists at the *Straits Times*, the *New Paper* or *Today* demanding a better deal for her, no account of her sad life that came to such a tragic end. No sympathetic commentary from the *Straits Times* writer Ken Kwek who, at the time Nguyen was hanged, argued that the mandatory death penalty at least should be reassessed, though not all uses of capital punishment:

> Perhaps in the months ahead, when emotions have died down, the mandatory death penalty—meaning its case-by-case, crime-by-crime application—should be reassessed by lawyers, officials and citizens alike. If that happens, we should all focus on the specific—how the mandatory death penalty might be removed for certain crimes—rather than fall for the broad-brush rhetoric calling for its complete and unconditional abolition.

Yen's case was reported only briefly in the local press and there was no official general discussion about the merits of capital punishment or comparisons to the way others, more fortunately placed in society, had been treated. It would have been an ideal topic for one of those late evening or Sunday afternoon round table television discussions with a variety of ordinary people saying their piece. There was no top-level wheeling and dealing with high-powered lawyers to save her young life—no chance of 'Rehab, Renew, Restart' for her.

'Yen May's life was tragic in so many ways but I don't believe enough was done for her to give her another chance in life,' said a friend of the condemned woman. 'She may have been a difficult case when attempts were made to rehabilitate her, and there were some when she was younger, but the authorities gave up on her too soon. She was disposed of like a piece of garbage. The break-up of her family devastated her and she turned to drugs to escape from reality. She was not a major trafficker, either, and the profit from what she sold was only to fund her own cravings, not out of greed to enable a super luxury life like the drug barons are able to lead unmolested by the law.'

But there was at least one happy moment she experienced shortly before she was hanged. She made her only sister promise to make the white wedding gown she had always dreamed of as a young girl and dress her in it before placing her body in her coffin. She got her wish. 'She looked beautiful,' said her friend, who, with tears streaming down her face, helped push Yen's coffin into the furnace.

20

WHITHER SINGAPORE?

Although some anti-death penalty activists in Singapore feel change is coming, a wider jury is still out on that question. Activist Alex Au and others reckon that the death penalty itself will never be abolished while countries like China and the United States lead the way in retaining it. 'Singaporeans are born to follow, not born to lead,' he says. 'This is a copycat society, which is not at all innovative, and they might follow these powerful leaders.'

However, many believe that the more controversial mandatory death penalty will eventually be struck from the statute books. It may still take a long time, judging by past and recent events, but the slow drip of pressure from within and outside Singapore will eventually result in a stream, then a river, which will sweep in the kind of changes that the people of Singapore desperately need. But the change they hope for is not just the abolition of the death penalty. It is also about freedom of speech and thought and the ability to express themselves in public—in peaceful demonstrations, by taking part in or watching television debates the likes of which they have in most countries on all kinds of sensitive issues, including crime and punishment, and even through the publication of books like *Once a Jolly Hangman*. Perhaps one day this will become the norm, and they will live their lives without anyone eavesdropping on them or reporting them to the authorities.

Even though the lawyer, abolitionist and human rights campaigner M. Ravi has been relentlessly vilified, he continues to fight on and is optimistic that at least the most heinous mandatory death penalty law is on its way out.

The Singapore Democratic Party also feels their voice is being listened to by a wider audience—if not by the PAP-controlled government. In 2005 the party organised a public forum to bring attention to the execution of Shanmugam Murugesu, convicted of trafficking 500 grams of cannabis. Chee Siok Chin, one of the organisers, said, 'We are glad to see that since then, the campaign against the mandatory death penalty for drug peddling has grown.'

Things got better at the UN General Assembly in 2007, two years after the Shanmugam Murugesu campaign began making waves. Singapore put itself at the forefront of nations opposing the call for a worldwide moratorium on executions. However, the island state found itself isolated when on 18 December 2007 a resolution calling for this was resoundingly approved.

The spirits of all activists were again boosted by a hard-hitting report in July 2008, when the International Bar Association (IBA) Human Rights Institute condemned Singapore for its lack of freedoms of expression, assembly and the press, and of the independence of the judiciary. The report, 'Human Rights, Democracy and the Rule of Law in Singapore', listed eighteen recommendations, urging the government to implement as a matter of priority. Mark Ellis, Executive Director of the Association, said, 'As one of the world's most successful economies, Singapore should be a leader in human rights and the rule of law, and should now have the confidence and maturity to recognise that this would be complementary, not contradictory, to its future prosperity.' He said Singapore falls far short of international standards in many areas. In particular, democratic debate and media comment are extremely restricted and government officials have initiated numerous successful defamation suits against both political and media critics. And this is the point. The egregious record of

Singapore in relation to the death penalty cannot be separated from its deeply embedded structures of authoritarianism and political illiberalism.

But most Singaporeans—if they were even aware of the conference and the IBA report—are not expecting dramatic change any time soon, despite the efforts of many influential lawyers at home. Those who felt hopeful soon had their dreams dashed. In March 2009, as if sending a loud raspberry to the IBA, parliament passed a new *Public Order Act* 'to create a more effective legal framework for Police management of public order'. The Act 'empowers police to effectively intervene, defuse and de-escalate dynamic situations on the ground with options to calibrate such interventions in an appropriate, measured and balanced manner'. Beneath the veneer of jargon and doublespeak this is actually yet another erosion of precious civil liberties.

Then, in October 2009, more than a year after the IBA report was released, Singapore's Supreme Court threw out an appeal by the *Far Eastern Economic Review (FEER)* in its defamation case involving Prime Minister Lee Hsien Loong and Minister Mentor Lee Kuan Yew. The publication had been found guilty of defaming the two leaders in an article published in the August 2006 issue, which quoted Chee Soon Juan, secretary general of the Singapore Democratic Party. *FEER* had appealed the verdict, but judges Chan Sek Keong, Andrew Phang Boon Leong and Judith Prakash dismissed the appeal with costs. They agreed with the earlier judgment that the words used in the article, written by its editor Hugo Restall, were indeed defamatory to both Lees.

Today Singapore is an extremely wealthy, globalised city-state. But far from giving its political elite the 'confidence and maturity' to open up the political system, to tolerate dissent and criticism and to protect fundamental human rights, the PAP government has actually chosen to go in the opposite direction. It has solidified its near monopoly on the political apparatus of the State by perverting the rights guaranteed in the Constitution through the passage and arbitrary enforcement of unconstitutional domestic laws. The absence of independence in a compliant judiciary and a media silenced through state ownership and the ever-present threat of defamation and libel suits has created a climate for the suppression of basic political freedoms. And in that context there is simply no meaningful debate about the death penalty and its repercussions.

For a brief time in early 2010 things looked like they might be getting better. In a stunning decision, Judge John Ng acquitted leaders of the Singapore Democratic Party who were charged with taking part in an illegal procession on 16 September 2007. Judge Ng said the walk 'did not cause inconvenience to the public, affect traffic flow or make noise which disturbed the public peace'.

The SDP leaders—Gandhi Ambalam, John Tan, Chee Siok Chin, Charles Tan and human rights activist Chong Kai Xiang— were marking the first anniversary of the World Bank/International Monetary Fund protest. The five, who were wearing T-shirts with the words 'Democracy Now' and 'Freedom Now' with a picture of a lighted candle, had walked from Speakers' Corner along North Bridge Road to Parliament House then along Bras Basah Road to the Istana—the presidential palace—then along Orchard Road to Queenstown Remand Prison. They were also conducting a vigil for Chee Soon Juan, who was in prison at that time for speaking in public. The group was charged with conducting a procession without a permit.

In his ruling Judge Ng dismissed the prosecution's 'simplistic' interpretation that a group of five or more people walking from one point to another in a public place to commemorate an event constitutes a 'procession'. He concluded that the five had not caused any public order offence. He seemed to vindicate the defendants' claim that taking part in processions and assemblies in Singapore is part of the fundamental rights of citizens provided for in the Constitution as well as the Universal Declaration of Human Rights.

But on 17 March 2010 hope turned to despair when High Court Judge Choo Han Teck reversed the judgment on the appeal by the Attorney-General. The High Court sent the case back to Judge Ng and he was pressed to impose fines or a jail sentence.

By pure chance a few weeks later I happened to bump into Gandhi Ambalam walking along a street in Kuala Lumpur. We went for coffee and he told me that because he refused to pay the S$2000 fine he must now go to jail for two weeks instead. Just as humiliating for a loyal citizen of Singapore, he had to apply to a judge for permission to cross the border to Malaysia to attend to some personal business. The next time I saw Mr Ambalam was when he arrived in a court room wearing an orange jumpsuit, handcuffed and shackled as though he were a terrorist or armed bank robber. In fact, he had been brought from Changi Prison where he was serving two weeks for taking part in another peaceful demonstration. He was fined again and jailed again because the fine was beyond his means. When asked by the judge how he pleaded to the charge, Mr Ambalam said to a hushed court room: 'I am the Chairman of the Singapore Democratic Party. My colleagues and I are citizens of this country and not slaves without any rights to be dragged before you. The charges that we face are in complete violation of our basic rights to freedoms of speech, assembly and expression that are enshrined in our Constitution.'

It made no difference. Such freedoms are not to be enjoyed by opponents of the People's Action Party. A few years earlier, activist Seelan Palay, the twenty-four-year-old maker of *One Nation Under Lee*, a forty-minute video narrating the rule of Singapore by Lee Kuan Yew, was called in for questioning by the police after a screening at a private function at the Peninsular-Excelsior Hotel. I happened to be there when the police and Media Development Authority barged in and seized the video. Since then it has been doing the rounds on YouTube, attracting tens of thousands of views. Seelan Palay was still under investigation for another 'offence' for screening the video while I was on bail in Singapore awaiting trial. In August 2010 he went to jail for two weeks for taking part in a peaceful demonstration outside Parliament House with other activists including members of the Singapore Democratic Party.

Martyn See, another Singaporean film-maker, has also become a victim of government witch-hunts. In July 2010, just days before my arrest for statements made in the first edition of this book, See was ordered to remove a political film from YouTube or face up to two years in prison and a S$10,000 fine. The film, called *Ex-Political Prisoner Speaks Out*, is the first ever public talk by Lim Hock Siew, a doctor and leftist who was held without trial from 1963 to 1982. But See said the order had come too late. Dozens of anonymous citizens had downloaded the film and it was spreading like a virus throughout the world. He said he reminded everyone that it is a criminal offence in Singapore to possess or distribute the film, but he had no wish, nor the means, to hinder them. He also told the authorities, who declared the work against the 'public interest', that ownership of the film belongs to all citizens of the Republic of Singapore.

'The film gives a distorted and misleading portrayal of Dr Lim's arrest and detention under the *Internal Security Act* (ISA) in 1963,' said a spokesperson. 'The Singapore government will not allow individuals who have posed a security threat to Singapore's interests in the past, to use media platforms such as films to make baseless accusations against the authorities, give a false portrayal of their previous activities in order to exculpate their guilt, and undermine public confidence in the government in the process.'

Having lived in Singapore for more than six years, making many good and brave friends along the way—and becoming another persecuted writer myself—I find it sad to approach the end of this book on such a pessimistic note. The tribulations of Gandhi Ambalam, Chee Soon Juan, John Tan, Siok Chin, Seelan Palay, Martyn See, myself and dozens more, might be considered trivial compared to other cases highlighted in previous chapters, but I hope these disturbing and shocking revelations—the kind the authorities are always desperate to cover up—will encourage Singaporeans to stand up, be bolder, think outside the box they have been confined in for far too long, bring about change and make their country really worthy of its reputation as 'Uniquely Singapore!'—that is, a world-class nation and not an Orwellian nightmare.

And whither Darshan Singh? Will he one day come to realise that his career of killing people on behalf of the State for almost fifty years was a complete waste of time, as did Albert Pierrepoint at the end of his long career? Only he will know. I wish him well. And I sincerely hope that, when his time comes, he too will go to a better place than this.

PART III

SCANDALISING THE JUDICIARY

21

MY ARREST

The loud banging began at around 6.30 on the morning of 18 July 2010. It might have started earlier, but if so I wasn't aware of it. I'd had only about three hours' sleep and was near-comatose.

'Who's there?' I finally mumbled sleepily.

'Police! Open the door.'

I was suddenly wide awake. Police? 'What do you want?'

'We have a warrant for your arrest!'

I thought I was dreaming. I was being arrested? I couldn't imagine why.

The launch of *Once a Jolly Hangman* the previous evening had been a tremendous success. The venue had been packed, with the crowd spilling into an ante-room and down the stairway. All kinds of people had turned up, about 150 in all, far more than the organisers expected. There were dozens of Singapore's growing band of human rights activists and opposition party members. Nora Murat of Amnesty International came down from Kuala Lumpur to make an impassioned speech in support of saving the life of another kid mule, Yong Vui Kong, then on death row for drug trafficking. Local opposition party members such as Dr Chee Soon Juan, his sister Chee Siok Chin, and John Tan and Gandhi Ambalam, were also in the audience. Rachel Zeng, who helped organise the launch, Seelan Palay, who has been jailed many times for his political 'crimes', and Andrew

Loh of the Online Citizen helped swell the numbers. Filmmaker Martyn See was there, too. A few embassy officials, including Julia Sutherland from the British High Commission, mingled with local and Malaysian lawyers and activists who had come to Singapore for one of the biggest death penalty protests ever seen in either country.

Teo Soh Lung launched her book, *Beyond the Blue Gate: Recollections of a Political Prisoner*, at the same time. A retired lawyer, she spent two years in jail under the *Internal Security Act* (ISA) in 1987 for being part of an alleged Marxist plot to violently overthrow Lee Kuan Yew and his PAP-ruled government.

I later found out that there were others attending had not been invited—police officers in plain clothes from the Internal Security Department posing as activists and sympathisers or reporters from the *Straits Times*. No matter who was there, however, my book had not been officially banned and we all felt reasonably safe.

Even Chong Ton Sin, my publisher and another victim of the political repression under the infamous ISA law, arrived from Kuala Lumpur. He had arranged for several thousand copies of the book to be delivered to Singapore several weeks earlier and it was flying off the shelves of all the major bookstores.

We'd had long consultations with the publisher in Kuala Lumpur and supporters in Singapore about how best to make the launch a success. Was I in danger of being arrested? I consulted well-known Singaporean Francis T. Seow, a former president of the Law Society and one of Lee Kuan Yew's right-hand men until he fell afoul of the government in 1988, forcing him to flee to the United States. His advice: as long as it's all correct, you have nothing to fear. As far as I was concerned it was all correct.

Chong helped stack copies of both books on tables at the Post Museum in Little India. They was selling fast and a long queue formed at another table where I was signing copies. The speech-making began. First local activist Alex Au, a fervent death-penalty abolitionist, took the microphone. He was followed by Nora Murat, who talked about the State-ordered execution of Vui Kong. Then I spoke about how I came to write the book and how shocked I was at the prosecutorial scandals I'd uncovered. So tragic and heart-breaking and unjust were they, I said, their stories often brought a lump to my throat. This was not the squeaky clean, decent and honest country I'd so often been told it was—but a perfect model of social engineering by an authoritarian government the likes of which had been tried before in many parts of the world—and failed. It was the stuff that inspired futuristic novels like *1984*, *Brave New World* and *Fahrenheit 451*.

Afterwards, some of us went for late-night supper in a Chinese restaurant nearby. We talked enthusiastically about the launch and how it fitted in perfectly with the campaign to save Vui Kong, news of whose imminent execution was beginning to reverberate across Southeast Asia and the rest of the world, but especially in Singapore and his home country, Malaysia. We never gave a thought to anything going amiss, especially as I had been allowed to enter Singapore from Penang where I was living at the time.

After supper I joined a young friend, Clara Tong, at a karaoke bar and we stayed until around 2.30 am drinking beer and singing all the songs we could handle without sounding too ridiculous. Actually, Clara has a great voice and picked a favourite for me to sing just before we left: Sinatra's 'My Way'. It seemed to fit my mood. I received a round of applause for my impassioned rendition—not realising at the time that two plain-clothes Criminal Investigation Department (CID) officers were also in the bar playing pool and secretly watching my every move. Then I returned to my hotel near City Hall and Clara went home by taxi.

I'd slept heavily until the knocking on the door began. I staggered to the door in shock and again demanded to know who was there before I opened it.

'We are police officers from the Criminal Investigation Department. We have a warrant for your arrest.'

'What are you talking about? What have I done?'

'We'll explain later,' the voice replied. 'If you don't open it the manager will.' As I turned the lock and gingerly opened the door, four men in plain clothes poured in like commandos. 'Get dressed! Pack your clothes,' one of them ordered harshly. They hardly gave me enough time to pee and clean my teeth. 'Don't shut the door,' another told me as I entered the bathroom.

They ransacked the room, looked under the bed, ripped off the sheets, and inspected the cupboards and balcony. When I had stuffed all my possessions into my holdall—I'd brought just enough for a three-day trip—I was bundled down the back stairs to an unmarked car parked at a side entrance. I wondered for a stunned moment if they had mistaken me for a terrorist or armed bank robber. Moments later, sitting between two of the officers in the back seat, we were speeding towards the Central Police Headquarters bordering Chinatown. The officer who appeared to be in charge looked at me several times with a strange, self-satisfied smirk on his face, as though he had indeed caught a very dangerous person.

Inside the Central Police HQ all my belongings were taken away from me. I was forced to hand over my passport, mobile phones, wallet, cash and credit cards. Then they took my belt and socks. All I was left wearing was a thin T-shirt, pants and briefs. Everything was laid out on a table in front of me and photographed. Then I was taken to a large, brightly painted cell on the eighteenth floor. As I lay on the concrete floor, still stunned by my sudden arrest, I remembered joking with my eldest daughter, Kim, the night before the launch. I'd sent her a text message from a restaurant in Batu Ferringhi, near my home in Penang, to say I was having dinner before flying down to Singapore the next morning. 'Make sure it's a good one,' she replied. 'It may be your last for a long time!' She had been joking, of course, but she had read the book, which I'd sent her some months earlier, and was a little worried that I might be in trouble.

Unknown to me, as I lay on the floor of my cell, news of my arrest had spread like wildfire. The headlines screamed: 'British Author

Arrested in Singapore.' The British Broadcasting Corporation's (BBC) report went around the world with every hourly news bulletin. The wire services—Agence France-Presse (AFP), Associated Press (AP), Reuters and Germany's Deutsche Presse-Agentur (DPA) also buzzed with the story. But at that time I had no idea what was happening beyond the walls of police HQ. At one point, a friendly CID officer standing guard outside popped his head around the door and said with a broad grin: 'You are news all over the world!'

After breakfast of cold rice and overcooked veggies in the cell, a young prison guard opened the cell door, handcuffed me and took me to a small office where my prescription drugs were being held. As I took the morning dose, it occurred to me again that they really must have made a mistake. They really did think I was a dangerous terrorist, not a harmless old man who had merely written a book! Perhaps they thought I was connected to the Indonesian-based terror group Jemaah Islamiyah (JI)—responsible for the Bali bombings in 2002 and 2005. It was true I'd been in and out of Bali and Jakarta about twenty times over the previous five years. Maybe that had raised their suspicions.

A few minutes later, I was taken to another room on another level below the cell block. A sign on the door said 'Interview Room: Do not disturb'. There was a desk in one corner close to a huge glass panel. I suspected someone was watching and perhaps video-recording the proceedings in the adjoining room. I had read Francis Seow's book *To Catch a Tartar* which described a 'cold room' in which Seow had been tortured. But I never dreamed that one day I would be held inside just such a room and be interrogated myself. The room was very cold and the temperature seemed to drop every minute.

Three documents were thrust into my hands. I glanced at them, barely comprehending what they meant. One said 'Order of Committal' and 'contempt of court' and 'acts in connection with the bringing into existence the publication and distribution' and 'scandalised the Singapore Judiciary'. The two other documents detailed two other charges with the words 'criminal defamation' and 'illegal communication', both offences under the *Official Secrets Act*. It was all becoming very clear. It was about my book. They had not mistaken me for a terrorist after all!

The questioning began. 'Are you the author of this book?' asked CID Special Investigator Kelvin Kwek. He had a copy of *Once a Jolly Hangman* in front of him at an angle so we could both see it the right end up.

'Yes,' I said. I could see yellow stickers jutting out from almost every page.

He turned to a certain page in the middle. 'Are you the author of that paragraph?'

I glanced at it. 'No, that's in a report by the International Bar Association. It fits nicely with the next paragraph—a statement by Amnesty International.' The purpose of quoting them, I explained, was to support my claim and that of many abolitionists that the death penalty is disproportionately imposed on the marginalised in society, especially the lowly, often simple-minded mules, while the wealthy, the privileged and well-connected are given more favourable treatment.

As I spoke, Special Investigator Kwek tapped away at a laptop, recording every word. He was wearing a buttoned-up shirt and jacket with the collar turned up. Not surprising, either. The room seemed to have become even colder. Just above my head was a vent and a jet of cold air was shooting down the back of my neck. I was beginning to feel extremely uncomfortable.

The questioning droned on and on, hour after hour. He turned the page and pointed to another sticker on another paragraph. 'Are you the author of that statement?'

'Yes.'

'Why did you write that?'

'I am telling a story about a poor Nigerian soccer hopeful who was lured to Singapore by a sophisticated adult to find a club which would enhance his career. Instead of realising his dream he was hanged for drug trafficking. Even the judge who sentenced him to death said in his findings that there was no evidence that he knew what he was doing—but that he should have! That was an appalling case to my mind. This eighteen-year-old should have just been sent back to Nigeria and advised never to trust adults like the one who tricked him! Or maybe they could have used him as bait to catch the big fish ...'

Officer Kwek tapped away. The pain in the back of my neck and general discomfort of the cold room were becoming unbearable. 'Look, this is making me ill. If you don't turn off the cold jet I will clam up. I'm cooperating because I have nothing to fear or hide. All I am doing is repeating what's in the book anyway. Just read it!'

He agreed to let me sit at the other end of the table, but it was still extremely cold. After several hours of further tedious questioning, I said, 'Why don't you just read the book? Then you will understand what it's all about. Why pick out so many odd statements here and there?'

He replied: 'I am just trying to get to know you.'

'Well, if you really want to get to know me, let's go to a nice bar near here on Neil Road. We can chat, have a beer and play a game of pool. I'm a hot-shot player. The locals around here know me by my nickname—Killer! That would be a nice way to get to know me instead of sitting here.'

He ignored my sarcasm and turned to another chapter where I'd quoted two retired Central Narcotics Bureau officers who had revealed some of the more sordid secrets of their work. 'What are the names of these retired officers? Where did you meet them? How did you get to know them? How old are they? Chinese? Indian? Malay? Describe them. Were they tall? Fat? Short?'

The machine-gun speed questions were giving me a headache but I gave nothing away. I didn't know their real names to start with. Instead I made up new ones so he could write something down. Had they told me their real names, even though I promised them anonymity, they would have been in danger of prosecution themselves. German journalist Hommy Dara was the link. He arranged the first meeting. It was done very discreetly.

'What's the name of this German journalist?'

Another false name: 'Fritz Heine.'

'Where did you meet him?'

'In Singapore.'

I was determined to be as vague as possible. He may have suspected I was lying and persisted with the rapid questioning. But I told him I was not prepared to break the journalists' code—never divulge a confidential source.

The questions continued hour after humourless hour with occasional bathroom breaks and for lunch and dinner or a cup of coffee or tea and biscuits that were in abundance in a kitchen just along the corridor.

I clocked up from ten to twelve hours every day from around 10.30 am on Sunday 18 July until Thursday 22 July at around midnight. Unknown to me, human rights lawyer M. Ravi had been busy arranging my bail with young activist Seelan Palay, who had been at my launch and volunteered to stand bail. Dazed and exhausted, I emerged from the police station at midnight on Monday 19 July—after almost two full sleepless days and nights feeling I had been through a wringer. It was explained that the bail was conditional—my passport had been confiscated, and I must return for daily interrogations starting at 10 am the next day. In the meantime I had to move from one hotel to another; the hotel where I'd been arrested refused to take me back. Without a passport this was extremely difficult, seriously adding to my stress and exhaustion.

At my launch I'd met Koh Hsiang Yu, a young woman who had given me a card describing her as a reporter from the Chinese language newspaper, *Lianhe Wanbao*. The next time I saw her she was coming out of police headquarters where I was being interrogated every day.

She had just handed over her tape recorder to one of the investigating officers and made a statement concerning my speech that she had secretly recorded and a brief interview I gave her after the event—not suspecting her real undercover job. The launch had been private, by invitation only, but it seems that some 'special' guests managed to wheedle their way past security.

After five dizzying days of interrogation and with worrying chest pains, I went to see my GP in Bukit Timah where I used to live. The results of the ECG alarmed her so much that she made an urgent appointment for me to see my cardiologist, Dr Peter Yan, at Gleneagles Hospital, whom I had also known since I moved to Singapore from the United States in 2003. He, too, was alarmed at the sudden deterioration in my heart condition. Until then it had been kept stable with a stent and a range of prescription drugs. I have always led a healthy, non-smoking, near-vegetarian lifestyle with daily exercise in the gym or long-distance walking—I have four finishers medals for walking half-marathons in under three hours, and I often took to the rugged trails at Bukit Timah Nature Reserve and MacRitchie Reservoir. More tests followed—an MRI, a twenty-four-hour heart monitor, three times on the treadmill in all. I was so wired up with electrical devices that my outside must have looked more like the inside of a robot! My GP and Dr Yan advised that the relentless daily interrogations should stop. A bemused Dr Yan said: 'If you have a heart attack and die in their hands it will be disastrous for Singapore!'

'It will be disastrous for me, too,' I added.

Investigator Kwek, however, had still not officially agreed that the interrogations should cease. I'm sure it was thought by his superiors that my medical problems were just a ruse to hinder the 'enquiries'. So I did not blame him. He was under the gun, too. But in the end he relented, following a complaint sent by Ravi to CID headquarters along with my medical reports.

During a break one evening, while going through my emails in an internet café, I saw a message from Justine Burley, a Canadian living in Singapore with her British husband. They had read of my plight and asked if I would like to have dinner with them one evening. At the time I was too concerned with finding a suitable place to live and couldn't accept the invitation. But, as if by magic, Justine must have sensed my problems—or she may simply have heard about them. Another email. This time it was an invitation to stay at their home. It was such a wonderful, heaven-sent gesture. It enabled me to rest, recover my strength and keep me balanced. At that time I was both angry over being treated in such a barbaric way and scared of what might happen next. I was told that I could be jailed for six months on one charge and two years on another.

From my temporary home I was able to respond to the many hundreds of emails from family, friends and supporters in Malaysia, England, the United States, Canada, the Netherlands, France, Germany and Indonesia. The outpouring of expressions of shock and disgust that Singapore had arrested me for writing this book was truly astonishing.

The first protests, of course, came from Amnesty International's officials and activists. I had known some of them for a long time, especially Margaret John in Canada who was responsible for monitoring human rights issues in Singapore and Malaysia. Messages of support came in from all over the world. Then came more strong protests and support from Reporters without Borders in Paris and London. Requests for interviews poured in from Sydney, Glasgow, Paris, Hong Kong and London. The BBC sent Rachel Harvey, one of its top reporters from Bangkok, for an exclusive interview. It went worldwide and was very critical of Singapore's lack of freedom. That got BBC staff in Southeast Asia into trouble with the authorities. From then on they were reminded they should stick to only nice, uncritical stories about Singapore—particularly about finance and its economic success. They were also ordered not to send reporters to cover my trial and preliminary hearings. Undaunted, Reuters, AFP and AP covered almost every event in the proceedings from beginning to end. The *Straits Times*, *Today* and the *New Paper* were represented, too. Bloggers were also having a field day on the internet. Their reports and comments added to an international chorus of protest. Special editorials and commentaries condemning Singapore were published in the *Guardian*, the *Wall Street Journal*, the *Economist* and *Christian Science Monitor*. They were backed up by Singapore's the Online Citizen, Temasak Review, Singapore Democrats, the Think Centre, the blogs 'Singabloodypore' and Alex Au's 'Yawning Bread', and exiled lawyer Gopalan Nair with his distinct daily barbs on the 'Singapore Dissident' blog from his home in San Francisco. My arrest and trial was also reported regularly by Channel NewsAsia, the *Straits Times* and *Today* as well as local Chinese, Malay and Indian language newspapers. Most carried photos of me arriving at or leaving the Supreme Court.

I'd suddenly become recognised everywhere I went. Many locals and expats gave me double looks, or shy waves of support. Many would approach me to shake my hand and wish me luck. A motorist pulled to the side of the road, wound down his window and asked: 'Are you Alan Shadrake?' Then he stuck his hand out to shake mine and said: 'Thank you so much for writing that book! I've just finished reading it.' He had taken the trouble to go to Johor Bahru, just across the border in Malaysia, where it was on sale and still on the best-seller list. On the street a taxi driver got out of his cab, shook my hand and said: 'I am very pleased to know you. This is my lucky day. I will tell my family as soon as I get home.' Then he hugged me. There were many more such instances—but one that particularly stands out was an evening that I was in a restaurant with friends. The waiter came to my table with a note. It was from a couple at a table on the patio. 'Hi Alan,' it began, 'thank you for speaking out for us and against the PAP. Your book has opened our eyes to the inner workings of the judicial system in Singapore and how it benefits the elites. God bless you and all the best in your court hearing.'

Facebook was also used as a major sounding board by Singapore's critics—mainly citizens in the country or living overseas in Australia, the United States, Britain and Southeast Asia. A photo of me giving a V sign as I entered the Supreme Court illustrated a 'Free Alan Shadrake!' wall, which was bombarded with dozens of wonderful, encouraging messages every day. YouTube fans spoke up on my behalf, too. The 'Hitler's Singapore' sketches were particularly funny. Using clips from actual movies depicting the final days of the German Nazi dictator and with subtitles in English, they lampooned those responsible for my arrest with an enraged Führer scolding his subordinates for not telling him *Once a Jolly Hangman* had been published and was being sold in Singapore bookstores. 'Who wrote it?' Hitler demanded in one scene. 'Some bugger from the UK,' was the reply.

Then things took a slightly sinister turn. I found I was being followed and watched everywhere I went. In a wonderful gesture of solidarity, Soh Lung helped me find another place to stay while I was awaiting trial. She warned me that my mobile phones—which had been returned to me after I was released—were now under surveillance. As we walked to a block of flats in Marsiling, near the Malaysian border, she noticed a young man behind us. He followed us into the lobby, got in the lift, then jumped out just as the door closed, saying on his mobile: 'Yes, it's Alan.' Soh Lung was not at all surprised. 'They are listening to every call you make,' she said calmly. 'They know we are in touch and coming here. Just be careful what you say from now on.'

I remembered the day Officer Kwek returned my mobiles to me. 'You will be better able to keep in touch while you are on bail,' he said. Little did I know then that the idea was to keep in touch not just with me but all my friends and associates. This kind of thing is nothing new to Singaporeans who stick their necks out. My first personal experience of this after my release happened when I called a journalist friend whom I'd known for many years. We'd long had each other's telephone numbers on our mobiles, but she panicked when I rang her soon after being released from custody, concerned about bugged phones. This was the first time I had come across this kind of fear since I'd lived in West Berlin during the Cold War. I had many friends on the communist side of the Wall who had told me about their relatives or colleagues suddenly disappearing and ending up in prison for political crimes. But, surprisingly, my journalist friend was not alone.

The cold treatment I received from some of my friends and colleagues was more than compensated for by all the warm collegial support I received around the world. On 31 August 2010, Jean-François Julliard, Secretary-General of Reporters without Borders and François Cantier, President of Lawyers without Borders (France), sent a strong letter to Holger Standertskjöld, Ambassador and Head of the European Union Delegation to Singapore. They wrote:

> We are extremely concerned about Alan Shadrake, a British journalist who is being prosecuted in Singapore on a charge of contempt of court in connection with his new book, *Once a Jolly Hangman: Singapore Justice in the Dock*, a well-researched critique of Singapore's judicial system and its use of the death penalty. However, Mr Shadrake's book contains no defamatory statements, personal attacks or verbal violence aimed at undermining the proper functioning of the judicial system. On the contrary, it is a scholarly critique of the system, its independence and its methods of working, which is the result of a great deal of research, in the course of which he met key participants in the system including its victims and executioner. It is absolutely vital that British and European representatives should be there, not only to protect a writer who just did a piece of journalistic investigation, but also to underline the European Union's commitment to freedom of expression and the principle of judicial transparency.

Support came from other quarters too. Jonathan Heawood, Director of English PEN, wrote:

In a modern country like Singapore, it is outrageous that someone can be prosecuted just for writing a book. The subject matter is clearly in the public interest and the people of Singapore deserve to read what Alan Shadrake has to say about their government. Unfortunately, colonial era laws of sedition and criminal defamation have allowed the government to victimise this seventy-six-year-old writer. Singapore simply cannot claim to be serious about democracy while it continues to make use of these outdated and illiberal laws.

Not all the comments were so serious though. Joe Mullins, a veteran journalist I have known all my professional life, sent me a message of hope from Florida: 'Don't worry Alan, if it takes us twenty-five years, we will get you out of there!' And my youngest daughter, Lydia, having heard the news of my arrest on the BBC, emailed: 'Will they hang you, Dad?'

'I don't think so,' I replied. 'But I am sure they would like to!'

22

MY TRIAL AND SENTENCING

My three-day trial in the Supreme Court was set to start at 10 am on Monday, 18 October 2010. The protests pouring in from all over the world set the stage for a kind of trial that had never been seen in Singapore history. International television crews and the print media were in full force outside the Supreme Court as I arrived with my lawyer. And they were there for the next two days, always waiting for the latest on-camera comment. As a veteran journalist, I never imagined for a moment that I would end up on the other side of so many cameras or have tape recorders thrust under my nose.

They were hoping I would come out with yet another 'defiant' outburst like the one I'd made at my first appearance in court several weeks earlier: 'I will not be cowed. I will not grovel. I will not say sorry.' My refusal to kowtow seemed to have won the hearts of many Singaporeans sick of being bullied and threatened if they raised their hands in protest. But my book was never intended to be a 'wholesale attack' on Singapore's judiciary, as Hema Subramanian, the Attorney-General's counsel, claimed. The subtitle of that edition was 'Singapore Justice in the Dock', not 'Singapore Judiciary in the Dock'—and the book had been praised as a legitimate critique of the application of justice, especially in the various cases I had investigated.

The court room was quiet as we waited for proceedings to begin. When Judge Quentin Loh arrived, Ms Subramanian set out the case against me for 'scandalising the judiciary': fourteen charges based on passages in the book. Ms Subramanian claimed they contained 'allegations and insinuations that the Singapore judiciary, in determining whether to sentence an accused person to death, succumbs to political and economic pressures, and that the Singapore judiciary lacks independence'.

My lawyer, M. Ravi, put up a stout defence. He said that apart from a slight error concerning sentencing guidelines in drug consumption cases (corrected in this edition of the book), I stood by my assertions. He then took the court through each of the passages from my book that Ms Subramanian had identified as being in contempt. He argued that none of the allegedly contemptuous items posed a risk, as Singaporeans are well educated and could assess for themselves whether the allegations made against the judiciary were 'fair and reasonable criticism'.

Some drama ensued on the third day of the trial when Ms Subramanian threatened Ravi himself with contempt of court. While rebutting my defence that nothing in my book could be construed as being in contempt, she told the court that she had been instructed to express regret over the many 'mischievous' and 'baseless' allegations Ravi had made since the hearing began.

She told Judge Loh: 'We do not want to deal with these unwarranted attacks here at this stage because we do not want to indulge in the tactics of the defendant of distracting the court from the issues before it.' She went on to say that Ravi had accused the judiciary of 'rubber-stamping' the contempt applications of the Attorney-General in the past.

Ravi stated his intention to discharge himself from the case if he was being threatened with contempt proceedings: 'There would surely be a conflict of interest if I continue acting for the author.' But Judge Loh cooled the atmosphere, telling Ravi that any applications to hold him in contempt would very probably come before the same court, which would be fully aware of the facts.

Ms Subramanian then took up her case again. She maintained that I had 'impugned the impartiality, integrity and independence of the courts by claiming that judges in Singapore favour the rich and privileged, and allow irrelevant considerations, such as trade and political considerations, to affect their decisions'. She also repeated my 'contemptuous' claim that the judiciary was compliant in the suppression of political dissent, ruining dissenters by awarding huge damages in defamation cases against opponents of the People's Action Party.

The court should not give any weight to arguments that Shadrake wrote the book from the view of the man on the street,' she said, adding: 'He is an investigative journalist and claimed to have written a well-researched book to expose the scandals of the Singapore judiciary.' She then said that my 'concocted scandals clearly undermined the authority of the courts'.

At the conclusion of the trial, Judge Loh found me guilty of contempt. The sentencing hearing was set for one week's time and Judge Loh offered me another opportunity to apologise. My answer was that two minor corrections would be made in future reprints or editions as explained—but that I would never disavow my book. I was heading for Changi Prison and a hard cell floor again.

When Judge Loh's judgment was released, it caused quite a stir among the legal community. The judge had departed from previous Singapore contempt cases where the 'inherent risk' test was used, preferring instead the 'real risk' test. He said:

A publication must pose a real risk of undermining public confidence in the administration of justice before it is held to be contemptuous ... First, a real risk ... must have substance, but need not be substantial. *A fortiori*, it is not necessary to show that public confidence was actually undermined by the impugned publication ... any degree of risk above the de minimis level, including 'a small likelihood', is a contempt, with the seriousness of the risk going only to mitigation.

Secondly, whether such a real risk is posed is eminently an objective question of fact to be determined in light of all the circumstances of the case, including the author and nature of the publication and the scope of its dissemination, and bearing in mind local conditions.

Judge Loh rejected the 'inherent tendency' test because 'inherent' means 'something intrinsic', suggesting that the context in which the statement is made and other external factors need not be considered. He also rejected this test because it appeared to cover publications that have no potential effect on public confidence in the administration of justice. Furthermore, Judge Loh felt that 'real risk' was more likely to be accessible to members of the public, who would need to understand the test in assessing the risk of contempt regarding their own behaviour. He emphasised that while the formulation had changed, the Singaporean 'inherent tendency' contempt cases decided between 1991 and 2009 would have had the same outcome—the facts of those cases would have also satisfied the 'real risk' test.

Lawyers and law academics interviewed by the *Straits Times* shortly after the judgment was released felt that it did not pave the way for a more relaxed view of contempt in Singapore because of the breadth of the 'real risk' definition.

On 16 November 2010, Judge Quentin Loh delivered his judgment on the eleven charges on which he found me guilty. I was sentenced to six weeks' imprisonment and a fine of S$20,000.

POSTSCRIPT

As this new edition of *Once a Jolly Hangman* goes to print, my case is still pending while I prepare to appeal my conviction and sentence at a hearing scheduled for 11 April 2011. But prosecuting me for writing this book has put Singapore and its justice system in the world spotlight as never before. That the Singaporean authorities decided to go after me says something about their judgment. By putting me in the dock they have done more to expose the horrors of capital punishment than I ever could, drawing public attention to the errors and manipulations that always attend this obscene barbarity anywhere it is still practised.

While the powers that be say they have not banned *Once a Jolly Hangman*, the first edition of this book cannot be bought officially in the Lion City. This enables its leaders to be able to say, honestly, that Singapore does not ban books. But if any bookstore or individual tries to sell any book they disapprove of, they come down hard. This is just what happened with three local activists—Seelan Palay, twenty-seven, Jarrod Luo, twenty-seven, and Rachel Zeng, twenty-eight. On 24 January 2011 this brave trio was summoned to the Major Crime Division of the Criminal Investigation Department and told they were under investigation for selling twelve copies of my book. If charged and found guilty they could end up in prison and heavily fined too. Of course, while suppressing books Singapore-style is not quite as dramatic as book burning, it is just as sinister.

The week before the Palay, Zeng and Luo investigation began, there was another battle in the fight for true democracy. Singapore's judiciary rejected long-persecuted leader of the Singapore Democratic Party Dr Chee Soon Juan's appeal against his convictions for speaking in public without a permit—incidents that date as far back as 2005. He was sentenced to a $20,000 fine or twenty weeks' imprisonment in default—and given six weeks to pay up or go to jail. 'The High Court's decision was not unexpected but its timing is unfortunate,' said Dr Chee's sister, Siok Chin, referring to the fact that the People's Action Party was in the midst of preparing for the imminent General Election, expected to be called any moment. 'With Dr Chee at its helm, the SDP has grown tremendously in the last few years,' said Siok Chin. 'It has attracted many credible candidates and energetic young people who are eager to help the party do well in the elections and serve the people. The PAP leadership is not at all happy at the growth of all the opposition parties in recent years and is worried as never before.'

Countless millions of people throughout history have died—and are still dying—for the natural-born right to freedom of speech and thought. In their deaths and suffering they have left behind a legacy of hope in places where hope had for too long been in short supply. And now there is in Singapore a small band of brave young activists willing to put their futures on the line and stand up and fight for these rights and real change. Such a miracle happened in East Germany in 1989 when the Berlin Wall came tumbling down. As a young freelance reporter I lived in Berlin for six years, almost from the time the Wall was first built in 1961, and I wrote a book about the ingenious ways people used to escape Communist oppression. A few years ago I saw *The Lives of Others,* a German film depicting those times. It finishes with actual newsreel scenes of the Wall coming down and the joy that everyone felt there and around the world. I would recommend that film to everyone who despairs that similar change will ever happen in Singapore and another kind of wall come down. It *will* happen.

ACKNOWLEDGMENTS

This book would never have been written without the invaluable help of many people. Perhaps the most important are some of Singapore's own human rights activists and abolitionists. There aren't many but their numbers are growing. These few brave men and women often provided me with vital information to help unearth yet another hidden legal scandal relating to someone's demise on the gallows. They helped expose what the authorities were afraid would leak out, thereby damaging Singapore's carefully protected, squeaky clean image. As I promised to honour their anonymity, I cannot name all of them. To do so would mean jeopardising their futures, as the Singapore authorities cannot tolerate any kind of dissent or criticism. These people could lose their jobs or even end up in prison—as many have done already and still do all too frequently. Some are parents of young children and I would not wish to see their livelihoods, liberty or dreams endangered in the way those of many other dissidents, critics and opponents of the government have been over the years.

There are others I cannot name but wish I could, including former officers of the Central Narcotics Bureau. Again, as promised, they must remain anonymous for now. But let's hope that one day in the not too distant future their names can be revealed and honoured.

Some people I can name and do so proudly. Firstly, I would like to thank a rare young man with real guts—the lawyer M. Ravi, a fearless human rights campaigner and abolitionist who fought long battles to try to save the lives of three young men from Singapore,

Malaysia and Nigeria and as a result became one of the most vilified citizens of Singapore, often subject to ridicule by the government-controlled *Straits Times*. He should be recognised as a hero and I would like to see his name one day on a road running alongside the Supreme Court: M. Ravi Avenue.

Although I met him only once, shortly before his death, I would also like to express my gratitude to Singapore's most illustrious human rights activist, the renowned lawyer Joshua Benjamin Jeyaretnam, or JBJ as he was affectionately known to his friends and supporters. Reading accounts of his fight for justice and decency throughout his entire lifetime inspired me to continue this quest. His brave, gutsy stance and lucid political and legal arguments should qualify him for inclusion on the list of Singapore's real heroes and I'd like to see his name gracing another auspicious thoroughfare.

I first discovered Alex Au on the internet via his blog, 'Yawning Bread', and later met him in person for several important interviews. My gratitude goes to him too. He is another veteran fighter for human rights and dignity.

I must also mention Dr Chee Juan Soon, who has been imprisoned, fined and sued for his efforts to bring about peaceful, democratic change to Singapore. No matter how long this malicious persecution continues, he will always stand on the moral high ground with his equally brave sister, Chee Siok Chin, and his ever-supportive wife, Mae.

The young activist Seelan Palay, who has been imprisoned himself, bailed me out of the police cell at midnight after my own arrest and has my heartfelt gratitude. Film-maker Martyn See, another fearless activist, should be acknowledged for attempting to record the opposition's view of history.

Two families of loved ones who were hanged agreed to cooperate with me to add even more devastating information to this book. Vasu Mourthi, his wife and three daughters welcomed me to their home in Ipoh, Malaysia, to talk about Vignes Mourthi, a loving son and brother. All of them decent, hard-working people, their lives were shattered by what happened to Vignes and they will grieve their loss forever. The citizens of Singapore might possibly have hung their heads in shame had they known the full facts of this young man's brutal end carried out in their name. The same goes for the family of Shanmugam Murugesu—his mother Madam Letchumi Ammah and his twin sons she helped raise in Jurong, Singapore. Madam Letchumi and these two brave youngsters did not hesitate to attend protest forums for many others who ended up on death row after their personal bereavement.

A Dutch social worker, Guus van Bladel, a permanent resident at the time of Maria Krol-Hmelak's arrest, was appointed her counsellor, attended her trial and was allowed to visit her on a regular basis throughout her incarceration. He kept a diary, invited me to his home in Malacca and allowed me to record many of the events that took place in the court room and during visits in her cell—an unusual privilege for someone who might well have ended up on death row.

Margaret John of Amnesty International fed me with endless, extremely useful information, which also confirmed much of my own personal research.

I must pay tribute to all those wonderful people who came to my aid after my arrest at dawn on 18 July 2010: Amnesty International's Secretariat in London—Louise Vischer, Lance Lattig and Hazel Galang; Margaret John and Nora Murat in Canada, Malaysia and Hong Kong; in New York, human rights activist Mickey Spiegel; in Paris and London, Heather Blake and Vincent Brossel of Reporters without Borders; Jonathan Heawood, director of English PEN, and author and member Victoria Glendinning who came to see me in Singapore with more messages of support; and Lord Anthony Lester who, with Heather Blake, brought my case into a debate on the death penalty in the British House of Lords.

I also acknowledge the generosity of international lawyer and human rights supporter Bob Amsterdam, and 'my' amazing London team of lawyers who freely supported M. Ravi from afar with important legal arguments in my defence: Ben Silverstone, John Jones, Parvais Jabbar, Edward Fitzgerald and Saul Lehfreund MBE. Saul and Parvais are co-founders and joint Executive Directors of The Death Penalty Project, based at Simons Muirhead & Burton solicitors in London, and are leading experts in the area of human rights and the death penalty.

I would like to thank the many hundreds of Singaporeans and expats who sent me messages of support—in particular the kindness and hospitality given to me by Justine Burley and her husband, Alan, and two other victims of political oppression: Teo Soh Lung, author of *Beyond the Blue Gate*, and her fellow 'Marxist conspirator', Souk Yee Wong. I will never forget any of you.

I am grateful too for the tireless campaigning on my behalf after my arrest that was carried out by Kristina Stockwood at IFEX, the International Freedom of Expression Exchange, and Gail Davidson of Lawyers Rights Watch, Canada.

I would also like to thank all of the hard-working and talented people at Pier 9 who have helped revise and update this book and bring it to a new audience. Thanks must also go to my dedicated and indefatigable agent, Sally Bird, and I extend particular gratitude to Julian Burnside for writing such an excellent and supportive foreword to this edition.

Last but by no means least—and strange as it may seem—I will be forever grateful for the kindness and hospitality of the 'star' of this book, Darshan Singh, perhaps the most extraordinary public executioner of all time. He is not the grim reaper of fantasy but a very likeable, down-to-earth man—like any other kindly father and grandfather. Although his calling was to kill people on behalf of the State, he did not do so callously but with gentle kindness and concern. I came to like him quite a lot—although not for what he did when he was master of the gallows.